Y0-EFP-846

Kirtley Library
Columbia College
8th and Rogers
Columbia, MO. 65201

The Role of the Buyer
in Mass Merchandising

THE ROLE OF
THE BUYER IN
MASS MERCHANDISING

Donald L. Belden

CHAIN STORE AGE BOOKS

An Affiliate of Lebhar-Friedman, Inc. New York

First published November 1971

THE ROLE OF THE BUYER IN MASS MERCHANDISING

Copyright © 1971 by Chain Store Publishing Corp., 2 Park Avenue, New York, N.Y. 10016. Printed in America. All Rights reserved.
Library of Congress Catalog Number: 70-181779
International Standard Book Number: 0-912016-13-2

658.72
BEL

01283

To My Wife Polly
and My Two Sons Brad and Jeff

Acknowledgments

I am indebted to many people for their help in the writing of this book. Publishing Director Marilyn Greenbaum has given invaluable aid and guidance throughout. Editor Tova Reich's professional assistance was most helpful. My son Brad helped me with the computer chapter and Daryl Cuppett with the chapter on importing. And Ralph Friedman got me started in the first place. Finally, my wife Polly has greatly expedited the project with her encouragement, her proofreading and her rare ability to decipher my handwriting.

Contents

viii

ix

of Merchandise; Price Advertising; Cooperative Advertising; Exclusive Arrangements with Vendors

The Buyer and the Consumer Movement

Buyer Qualifications: Background and Experience

The Buyer's Day

The Place of the Buyer in the Modern Retail Organization: Line and Staff Organizations; The Importance of Good Communications

Women as Buyers

Buyer Training: Preliminary Interview; Store Operations Orientation; Central Office Orientation

Advice to the New Buyer

Trends Within Retailing: The Big Will Continue to Grow Bigger; Planning Versus Scrambling; Electronic Data Processing

The Buyer of the Future

Foreword

The buyer's role in mass merchandising is *changing*. In this new decade of the '70s, it no more resembles the merchandising and procurement techniques of 30 years ago than a 1920 Ford takes after a '71 Mustang.

A lot is being said and written about these changes. Buyers for large national chains or smaller multi-unit operations are becoming marketing men, we're told. They're developing into quality control experts. They're using computers to track and trace the machine-gun motion of merchandise as it's sold. In the past 10 years, science has indeed replaced art in the merchandising field.

Yet for all these changes—accurately forecast and perceptive as they are—little is actually known about what a buyer really does. The job, the title "buyer," is dressed in a kind of glitter that makes it appealing to those inside retailing—and romantically alluring to the average person.

Everybody would like to be a buyer. Case in point: An executive for one of the nation's largest general merchandise chains not long ago asked a class of 250 high school seniors in Detroit which job they'd most like to have in retailing—and why? A full 85% said: Buyer. Why? "Because they take interesting trips all over the world. They travel in wonderful circles and meet exciting people."

The plain truth is, there's a wide gap between the image and the reality. Anybody who has ever visited a buyer's office in the heat of the average day—when he or she is being bombarded with calls or reviewing new items, samples and lines on a never-stopping treadmill—can attest to that.

And that's only one small fraction of a buyer's total job. What does the guy do? How does he do it? What considerations and judgments does he apply to his decisions? How do you buy merchandise?

There isn't any one definitive answer to these questions that wraps up the buyer-in-whole anywhere in print. Because merchandising as an art is still in a transitional stage and buying isn't quite yet a science, it hasn't been put together in any one place.

That's why this book by Don Belden is such a significant contribution to the retailing field in general, to mass merchandising in particular and to chain retailing more specifically. It fills the bill. It's an articulate, down-to-earth description of what a buyer does, how he does it, rich with the working examples of what goes into buying decisions and understandable explanations of the whys—written by a veteran of chain retailing who knows his way around all phases of buying as an art and as a modern science.

And, in the pages that follow, Don Belden also talks about the "new technologies" that will become even more important to the mass merchandise buyer of the oncoming '70s and '80s.

Today's buyers, he tells us, use computerized print-outs to track their sales motion and velocity—because competition and the consumer demand the right decisions faster. Many have almost instant-recall on an item as it's sold in a store or group of stores. Yet, ten years ago, the average buyer was bogged down and almost suffocating in paperwork, manual accounting systems and information-delays. Between the time sales reports reached them and the need for a reorder or a new "buy," they worked on instincts that were sharpened by years of store and field work—not to mention a finely-honed "feel" of the market.

Today, two basic elements are impacting the buying process as we know it and reshaping the responsibilities of the buyer himself: speed and volume.

Today's buyer must act and react with eye-blinking speed and certainty. He has to spot changes and catch trends on the rise. His decisions are no longer subject to a three-month incubation period, but more often to a few weeks, in some cases a few days.

And because of the mammoth growth of sales volume, buyers are specializing more—handling ever-narrower categories which require intense knowledge and technical expertise. A chain store buyer in this current decade, for example, will more and more become the master of 50 or 60 square feet within a single department that multiplies 50 or 500 or 2,000 times, depending on the number of stores in the chain.

The changes to come obviously will alter the buyer's role in mass merchandising even more dramatically than they have up until now. But one fact *won't* change: the basics of sound, aggressive, creative merchandising. The buyer who has mastered the fundamentals will be able to master the speed and the new technology mass retailers must control in years to come.

For everyone involved with chain retailing, whether they're in general merchandising, discounting, department stores or the non-foods areas of drug and supermarket stores, this book is must-reading and an important new reference for the thousands of suppliers and manufacturers who deal with buyers in today's changing mass-merchandise market.

Walter J. Schruntek
Editor/Publication Director
General Merchandise Editions of
Chain Store Age

Preface

The purpose of this book is to promote a better understanding of the buyer's varied and changing role. Newcomers to retailing and buying can use this book to gain insight into the buyer's function and into its relationship to all other phases of retailing. Experienced chain store buyers will find in these pages an exposition of their daily problems and of their colleagues' reactions to those problems. Marketing students with a special interest in retailing, or those seeking information about other marketing specialties, will find much of value here. For the manufacturer and his representative who sit across the table from the buyer and wonder what goes on in his mind and why he fails to see the merits of their matchless product, this book will hopefully clarify some of the buyer's puzzling and seemingly obscure decisions. And experienced retailers specializing in such areas as store management, financial and clerical administration, and other staff functions, will find that the description of the buyer's point of view provided here will add to their comprehension of the total retailing scene.

For all readers, we hope this book will help a little to bridge the serious communications gap between central buying offices and store management, manufacturers and retailers, staff and line personnel, controllers and merchandisers. As mass merchandisers become larger and larger, the trend toward greater specialization of function increases; and as functions become more and more specialized, the individual tends to narrow the focus of his interests. The result is a collapse of communication, understanding, and cooperation.

Language can also be a serious barrier to communication. The merchandiser may use trade jargon and abbreviations that are incomprehensible to customers and even to his own sales clerks; he, in turn, may be baffled by the computer language of the controller and his staff. It is hoped that this book will help to remove some of these roadblocks to mutual understanding.

Except for articles in some excellent trade magazines, surprisingly little has been written on the subject of mass-merchandise retailing. Obviously, the need for communication and the exchange of ideas is great. Not only is there a growing interest in business education in schools and colleges throughout the world, but there is also a spreading recognition of the fact that management training is a continuing career-long process.

We should also like to convey to all of our readers a sense of the excitement of buying and merchandising—the warm human involvement that is inherent in all phases of the ever-changing and ever-challenging retailing scene.

The Role of the Buyer
in Mass Merchandising

INTRODUCTION

The Mass-Merchandise Buyer

The typical buyer is a man past middle age, spare, wrinkled intelligent, cold, passive, noncommittal; with eyes like a codfish, polite in contact but at the same time unresponsive, cool, calm, and as adamantly composed as a concrete post or a plaster-of-Paris cast, a human petrification with a heart of feldspar, and without charm or friendly germ; minus bowel, passions, or a sense of humor. Happily they never reproduce and all of them go to Hell.

The above description of a buyer was written some 60 years ago by Elbert Hubbard, essayist, editor, and advertising man. His characterization might gain considerable support from a salesman who has just completed a series of unsuccessful visits to buying offices on a cold, rainy day.

In a calmer and less hostile mood, however, the mass-merchandise buyer would probably be portrayed as one who sits in judgment at the crossroads and helps to direct the traffic of goods from the producer to the consumer. His position is at the very heart of the retailing organization. He reviews an endless stream of merchandise flowing from manufacturers, and, from this stream, he diverts his selections to his company's stores in the right quantities at the right time.

THE EARLY CHAIN BUYERS

In the early 1900's chain stores developed rapidly and multi-store

1

operators were badly in need of helping hands. At first, partnerships were common; then corporations proliferated. Larger stores were built and branches were opened—near the original store at first, but soon spreading to distant locations. Buying and administrative headquarters tended to be centered in the merchandise and money markets of New York, Chicago, and Detroit.

As sales volume grew and the need for division of labor and greater specialization became apparent, buying by owners naturally gave way to chain store buying as we know it today. When five stores became fifty, the chain store founder quickly saw the advantages of delegating the buying to someone who had shown an aptitude for it and who would become an expert in that area.

Buying organizations grew without much design during those pioneer years. Typically, the most successful store managers would be given the opportunity to exercise their skills in a more specialized way for all the stores in their company. For example, they would help to administer a particular operation or to buy a group of merchandise for which they had perhaps shown a special flair or affinity. Their experience in store operations put them in a good position as buyers, giving them insight into what the stores could sell best. The buyer's role in the early chain store days was dominant, and he was usually quite effective. Armed with the power provided by his company's great purchasing advantages, he was able to bring to the consumer selections of merchandise that had never before been available so conveniently at such low prices. The public responded overwhelmingly.

Manufacturers also benefited from the success of chain stores. With new outlets springing up by the hundreds, they were able to contract with chain buyers for larger quantities over a longer period of time. This new security permitted the manufacturers to plan more efficient production, develop new items, and reduce both their costs and their selling prices. Together, both the manufacturer and the retailer learned how large-scale production and distribution work to their mutual profit.

But weaknesses in this buying system soon became apparent. Rapid growth led to a serious thinness at all executive and

2

supervisory levels, including buying. At first, busy top management was happy to leave most buyers pretty much on their own whenever reasonable competence had been demonstrated. But as chain store organizations matured and their officers had time to draw deep breaths and look about them, they came to realize that, in many instances, small buying kingdoms had grown up that were much too independent. Many buyers were very close to the founding officers and were profiting handsomely from stock ownership as the company prospered. The curtailment of the powers of these "merchant princes" and the assignment of some of their authority to others became quite a problem. The chains were now leaping forward and becoming more sophisticated in their approach to organization. The buyer who, in effect, had been running his own business within the larger business and had grown accustomed to dealing directly with top officers found it difficult indeed to see the need for further division of responsibilities or for the development of more specialized staff functions.

Problems Created by the Merchant Prince

One of the major problems created by the dominant buyer prince was his frequent disdain for teamwork and cooperation with other divisions of the company. His compensation was usually based directly on the growth of sales and profits in his merchandise category. The greater the attention, display space, and proportion of the company's investment he could obtain for himself, the greater his income and self-esteem. Struggles between buyers and merchandise managers were frequent, and overall company planning suffered. Sometimes two divisions of the same company bought practically the same merchandise and competed with each other. Rival buyers occasionally refused to communicate valuable data to each other. But top management persisted in its struggle to establish an efficient organizational structure. The need for specialization became more obvious as the size of each operation grew. And ultimately, the individualists became accustomed to the new way of doing things or they retired.

Sears, Roebuck and Company—A Case History

In 1918, a Sears executive made this statement: "Another feature of our organization is the confidence we place in the leaders of our departments. . . . Each department manager is given a large measure of responsibility in developing his department work according to his ability. The business is his business. He is not hedged with limitations, such as dull the initiative. The result is that these men have responded with their best. . . . We have applied the principles of democracy to a commercial enterprise."[1]

However, the depressions of 1920-1921 and the 1930's demonstrated to Sears' management the flaws in this federation-of-merchants concept. The quality of merchandise that appeared in the stores was very uneven. Each merchandise line was a reflection of the personal philosophy of the individual buyer rather than of the company. Some buyers preferred to buy low-priced goods while others leaned toward higher-priced products. As a result there was little consistency in the price appeal of various categories and a customer who had associated a particular Sears store with good-value, middle-priced electrical appliances might be at a loss when he found the lowest-grade floor coverings there. Obviously, Sears was presenting a mixed image to its customers. Manufacturers found themselves at the mercy of individual buyers and their whims. There was little centralized control over the size of assortments in the stores, and variety became immense as each buyer sought to get a bigger slice of the sales and display space.

Of course, all the chains were experiencing similar growing pains, but Sears was one of the first to tackle its problems by working out more advanced buying procedures. For example, the natural division of merchandise into the rough categories of "hard" and "soft" lines had come very early in chain development, but Sears very soon added a third category which it called "big ticket"—refrigerators, stoves, rugs, furniture, and other major appliances. Limited-priced variety chains—strictly five and ten, or five, ten, and twenty-five cent stores—had no need for a big ticket

[1]Boris Emmet and John E. Jeuck, *Catalogues and Counters, A History of Sears, Roebuck and Company* (Chicago: University of Chicago Press, 1950), p. 382.

category at that time but did have a third category called "variety," which consisted of such departments as notions, toilet goods, stationery, and candy. These variety departments organized the merchandising and display of a multitude of low-priced small wares in a convenient and orderly manner that had great appeal to consumers.

But whether the buying and merchandising was of big-ticket or of low-priced goods, the orientation was clearly toward the manufacturer rather than the consumer.

ORIENTATION TOWARD PROCUREMENT

Procurement of merchandise was the major problem in the early days. Manufacturers had to be found, convinced, and geared up to fill the huge and growing demand for all sorts of products. One of the reasons for this emphasis on the producer rather than the consumer was that the buyer encountered a hostile manufacturer, afraid of the effect of chain store competition on his established customers. The small druggist, grocer, or general store merchant saw the growing chains as a massive threat that would eventually gobble him up. He was quick to let his suppliers know how he felt about these new giant competitors and to bring pressure to prevent selling to them. Threats to boycott manufacturers who aggressively sought the business of the chains were effective at first, and hampered mass merchants from developing adequate selections of wanted goods. Many manufacturers also feared they would lose their power and dominance when forced to deal with giant retailers who had much greater purchasing leverage. In addition, the small independent merchant, with his grass roots political powers, was able to communicate his fears to his congressman. An era of anti-chain store legislation ensued that did not subside for many years, until mass merchandisers had won so secure a place in the hearts of consumers that support for such legislation simply died away.

Thus the problem of procurement tended to outweigh the importance of the skillful presentation of the merchandise to the customer. An excellent example of the thinking of the day was the merchandising of tinware, enamelware, and aluminumware.

5

Because the three came from separate industries it seemed natural not only to buy and reorder by industry, but to merchandise and display that way in the stores. Thus, as recently as the early 1940's, pails, double boilers, pots, pans, cabinets, water pitchers, coffee-makers, and chamber pots were merchandised by material rather than by end-use! Instead of displaying all coffee-makers together, for example, they were widely separated according to the basic material from which they were made. The grey enamelware was separated from the white, red or blue enamelware, which was separated from tinware and aluminumware. Obviously, the buyer was more concerned about the purchasing and delivery of his goods than he was about their sale and customer preferences. This sort of thinking permeated buying and merchandising until it gradually gave way to more modern display techniques as competition forced more attention on the customer's point of view.

ORIENTATION TOWARD CUSTOMER SATISFACTION

Sears was again in the vanguard in this new orientation toward customer satisfaction. Quality and value became primary aims of top management. As chain volume became more important to manufacturers, buyers were able to exert a stronger voice in the manufacturer-retailer relationship. Chain buyers began to specify the products they wanted from the manufacturer rather than to merely passively select one or more items from a larger number presented by the vendor's salesman. This "specification" type of buying was highly developed by Sears to the point where the company designed products and calculated costs and profits in advance of buying. Sears' innovations in scientific buying served as a model for other retailers. The opportunity for specification buying evolved as the chains became larger and larger scale buyers were able to guarantee the manufacturers markets for specially developed products.

In turn, improvements in buying techniques helped increase sales for the chain outlets. The achievement of big sales volume, so essential to the chain store system, was heavily dependent on large-scale and expert buying. The opportunity to sell large quantities of

6

merchandise attracted the finest manufacturers and encouraged their best efforts at their lowest prices. Skilled buying in such a favorable climate could only result in the best possible selections of attractive merchandise that would draw customer traffic and leave ample margins for a satisfactory return on investment.

But the buyer, in a sense, is both buyer and seller. He purchases on as favorable terms as possible from the manufacturer and then proceeds to "sell" what he has purchased to his merchandising superiors and store organization by seeking their approval and cooperation. His role is highly diversified and fast-changing. As we shall see, it is also challenging and interesting.

1

The Buyer-Vendor Relationship and the Middleman

No matter where you turn, it seems, manufacturers and suppliers are thinking like retailers—and vice versa—because they see today more than ever before that they are partners in the distribution of merchandise. Both have to plan sales to make profits. Both have to pay more attention to research in the marketplace and to the motives that make customers buy![1]

A key point in the entire distribution process is the confrontation between the buyer and the vendor. The smooth flow of merchandise from the factory to the consumer and all the careful planning of the manufacturer may be frustrated unless the buyer buys and the vendor sells with skill and understanding. The retailer, too, may lose the potential profits for which he is maintaining an expensive staff and store if the buyer-vendor relationship fails.

But the importance of the confrontation between the buyer and the vendor agent will vary according to the organizational setup of the particular buying and selling companies. It will depend on the amount of authority delegated by the manufacturer to his representative and by the retailer to his buyer. But even those buyers and vendor agents who have little individual authority in giant organizations are significant as communicators and interpreters.

The horse-trading, David Harum, aspect of buying, where the

[1]"Editor's Note," *Chain Store Age, Variety Store Edition,* April 1968, p. 35.

buyer and seller each attempt to outwit the other, has always been less important than imagined. Today the trend is more and more toward cooperative relationships. The competent buyer now comes to his interview with the vendor well informed on his model stocks, his store's display and promotional opportunities and limitations, and, through electronic data processing, the up-to-the-minute details of his operation. Presumably the vendor agent will come to the meeting equipped with comparable knowledge and equally sophisticated data.

HISTORY OF THE BUYER-VENDOR RELATIONSHIP

Buyers and vendors have not always been as cooperative or as scientific in their methods as they are today. The introduction to this book noted that manufacturers considered the early mass merchandisers a threat to the very existence of their traditional outlets, and were reluctant to sell to even the largest of them. The early chain buyers had to seek eagerly to convince unwilling suppliers to sell to them.

Even the manufacturers of highly advertised drugs, foods, and housewares, who depended on the widest possible exposure of their products to make their advertising profitable, were slow to break away from traditional distribution patterns. Appliance makers held out for a while against the discount chains, and soft goods manufacturers, particularly those with known, popular brands, held out even longer. But as mass merchandising and discounting won greater popular acceptance, manufacturers found it more and more difficult to resist the opportunity for increased volume.

During those early days chain retailers themselves had not yet decided what they would or would not merchandise, and manufacturers had not yet developed the full, comprehensive lines they now have. Chain store buying largely consisted of purchasing one item at a time or lots or closeouts, and browbeating duels over a single transaction were not uncommon. Gradually, however, a sensible teamwork approach to buying and selling replaced these muddled and unrewarding contests. The transformation to today's ideal of cooperative, programmed buying is a tribute to the growing skills of both the manufacturers and the mass merchandisers.

10

Sears, Roebuck and Company was probably the first large retailer to take aggressive, top-management action to establish continuity and better cooperation between its sources and itself. Former president Donald Nelson, as early as the 1930's, "sought to persuade sources that Sears, Roebuck was not interested in becoming a manufacturing colossus and swallowing up independent manufacturers. . . . He also sought to persuade sources that Sears was interested in their problems and in their continued profitability. . . . Nelson insisted that sources had to be considered by the company as a vital part of its structure, to be assisted in every possible way, to be given greater leeway when they had established their reliability . . . and that sources had a mighty contribution to make to Sears if their full enthusiasm could be aroused and unleashed on the problem at hand."[2] The tremendous growth and profitability of Sears over the years indicate that "this rapport has paid handsome dividends."[3] All mass merchandisers today are fully aware of the benefits that can accrue from teamwork with vendors, and their buyers are schooled in building and maintaining such synergistic relationships.

THE VENDOR'S RESPONSIBILITY TO THE BUYER

"Buyers respond to the professionalism of salesmen. Business relationships are *people* relationships, and they are successful when one emotion reaches out to another . . . and finds the warmth of acceptance."[4]

Professionalism is evidenced by the vendor who knows his product and its market thoroughly. The buyer will not only appreciate learning about the product's strong points, he will also value any information on its competitive position and merits. Since very few new products break through into previously undeveloped markets, and many are merely copies of items already available, the vendor must be able to offer improvements or price differentials that will appeal to the buyer. The professional vendor agent will have acquainted himself with the buyer's requirements as to timing

[2]Emmet and Jeuck, *op. cit.,* p. 403.
[3]*Ibid.* p. 410.
[4]Ben Gordon, "Editor's Note," *Chain Store Age,* July 1969, p. 27.

and optimum quantities for maximum sales and turnover. He will come prepared with the best available deal to fit the retailer's promotional schedule. From persistent store visits, he will understand the display and packaging problems at the point of sale and be in a position to help solve them for the buyer.

The skilled vendor representative will be attuned to the buyer's needs and problems. He will know why the buyer makes the decisions he makes—why he says yes and why he says no. He will understand the framework within which the buyer operates, and how it may differ from one type of retailing operation to another. He will recognize the retailer's need for turnover and the restrictions placed upon the merchandiser by investment budgets. He will tailor his company's offerings to fit the ordering procedures of the buyer's firm. He will know a great deal about the transportation costs of his wares and the precise delivery times to and from various areas, thus helping the buyer to schedule merchandise arrivals. And he will assume responsibility for the delivery of merchandise as planned. With a clear picture in his mind of the buyer's stores, their display fixturing, and their types of customers, he will offer appropriate packaging and display material. The buyer will appreciate, seek out, and tend to purchase more from the vendor who strives for their mutual advantage from a long-range point of view. The vendor who understands that pure "item" selling without any frame of reference is being replaced by a broader programming in which servicing buyers and their stores is as important as selling to them is likely to enjoy a wider and more faithful patronage by retailers.

Understanding Selling and Packaging Problems

The buyer will expect the manufacturer and his sales representative to fully comprehend what the rising costs of store operations have led to—the shortage of trained personnel and, most important, the trend to self-service. Buyers and vendors who plan to merchandise a line or item which requires more than the absolute minimum of store personnel assistance are doomed to fail in mass-merchandise outlets.

12

In the absence of trained sales personnel, packaging must do the selling job. The package must be durable enough to survive rough handling and be as pilfer-proof as possible. It must be of a shape and size that conserves space but still commands the customer's attention. Cartons must be labeled or illustrated for easy handling and quick identification at warehouse and store.

The size of the carton and the quantity it contains are vitally important. Suppose the buyer and the vendor representative are faced with an item that the manufacturer has packed 36 pieces to a carton because this is the most economical unit to put together at the factory. If the sale of this item in the average store of a mass-merchandising chain is 12 pieces per month, and if this 36-pack has no inner pack (in other words, the 36 pieces are not in 6- or 12-piece inner packs which could be conveniently removed and shipped to stores individually), the store would be forced to reorder 36 pieces or none. Alternatively, the warehouse would be saddled with the high cost of unpacking the carton and reshipping individual pieces. At the proven rate of sale of 12 pieces per month, a store's commitment on the item (12 pieces on hand and 36 pieces now ordered) would total 48 pieces, or a four month's supply. If the store reordered the 36-piece carton, it would have an unsatisfactory turnover rate, and, possibly, a greater storage problem; and if it waited to reorder until the next month, an out-of-stock condition would probably result. The obvious solution to this little problem is a 12- or 24-piece pack, even at the higher costs it would necessitate. A good working relationship between buyer and vendor will identify and work out such problems as they occur.

Helping the Buyer Do His Job

The vendor representative who respects the buyer's tight schedule will be appreciated and favored. By marshaling his facts and presenting them clearly and concisely, the vendor agent will help the buyer organize his thoughts and decisions so that he can effectively "sell" them to his divisional merchandise manager or buying committee. The vendor representative who has not really considered, or who does not fully understand, the retailer's operation often does not have the needed information at hand, fumbles through his samples case to find it, and may in the end be forced to call back. Figure 1 is an example of a standard information form for vendors. The vendor representative should fill it out completely, thereby providing the buyer with many of the basic details he will need to evaluate the product and make a decision.

If the vendor has prepared an extensive advertising portfolio, the buyer should be forewarned and the presentation tailored to the available time. The alert vendor agent will sense how much time the buyer can spare for the social amenities and will not outstay his welcome. The vendor representative can make himself extremely valuable to the buyer by frequenting his stores, studying them closely, and reporting facts that are pertinent to the buyer's responsibilities and of which he may be unaware.

Keeping Up with Change

The buyer will cultivate and prefer the vendor who keeps up with or ahead of the changing patterns of distribution. The vendor who understands the impact of the computer and the fresh, accurate information it places in the hands of the buyer will be sought out. When details on the current rate of sale are known by the buyer, the vendor must talk unembroidered facts. Performance, or a program to improve performance, is of the essence; strictly personal relationships tend to become less important at such times.

To maintain or to improve his favorable position with a retailer, today's forward-looking vendor agent will follow through to make sure his products are selling at the store level. Such careful analyses by the vendor representative may result in sales aids, new displays and other types of in-store services, or in better deliveries, improved packaging, or a shift in advertising direction. Close attention to product movement may lead the vendor to convince the buyer that a different size or assortment will produce better results in general, or in a selected area or store size. This type of open communication between buyer and vendor is vital in today's fast-moving retail scene and will, through its mutuality, discover fresh, profitable opportunities as they evolve.

14

The Buyer-Vendor Relationship

FIGURE 1   Vendor New Item Form

(to be filled in completely by the vendor representative when
presenting a new item to buyer)

Date_____

Firm Name_____

Address_____

Telephone Number_____

Item Name and Number_____

Item Description—Size, Assortment, Color, Packaging_____

_____

Cost per Unit of Quantity Ordered_____

Recommended Retail Price_____

Is Item Prepriced?_____

Shipping Packing_____

Shelf Packing_____

Weight per Unit of Quantity Ordered _____

Shipping Points if Other than Above Address _____

Minimum Shipment _____

Availability Date of First Shipment _____

Normal Time Required to Ship Reorders_____

Cash Discount _____

Quantity Allowance_____

Advertising Allowance_____

Freight Allowance_____

Warehouse Allowance_____

_____
Signature of Vendor's Representative

15

THE BUYER'S RESPONSIBILITY TO THE VENDOR

Knowledge of Merchandise

The buyer must bring a reasonable knowledge of the merchandise to his relationship with the vendor. Though it is not necessary to memorize the exact ingredients and chemical composition of many kinds of merchandise, the buyer must understand how the product fits into his existing assortments, display space, and investment budget, as well as its market in relation to his store outlets. The buyer also has an obligation to know what the competition is offering so that he will be in a position to understand and appreciate the merits of the vendor's product.

Open-Mindedness

If and when the buyer lacks specific merchandise knowledge as well as an understanding of the exact place of the product in his particular retailing setup, he should be receptive and open-minded to the vendor's story. Whether or not he eventually purchases the item, the buyer can learn a great deal from listening to reports of comparative figures, the accomplishments of the competition, and the objectives of the vendor's promotional and advertising program. Vendors complain, with some justification, of the rigidity of buyers and buying programs, of investment and budget restrictions that leave little or no room for innovation and fast-developing sales opportunities. Vendors are also often frustrated by hard and fast retailer rules that prohibit any type of "missionary" work at the store level or the use of selling displays that do not fit into a strictly prescribed pattern. Today's fast-changing retail kaleidoscope demands buyer-vendor flexibility in all areas.

Good Communication

The vendor dealing with a buyer who is both knowledgeable and receptive will also wish to improve communication in order to implement joint actions and programs. When of sufficient importance, meetings between vendors and buyers may take place at the officer level, but long-term goals with major suppliers should be

16

set and reviewed at least annually at whatever level. The buyer-vendor relationship will flourish when there is scheduling for an even flow of orders and deliveries—when the panic button is not pushed regularly because of spasmodic ordering and unplanned promotions—and when a mutual, close relationship concentrates on major opportunities and avoids the trivial.

Selling to His Superiors

The effective buyer must also be a salesman of his buying decision. The authority of the buyer, or that of the buyer plus his immediate superior, varies greatly among mass merchandisers. In some cases the buyer's decision is final or rarely subject to change, but even buyers with maximum authority find it important to develop selling ability.

However, as the average retail chain grows, its management is more likely to review buying decisions and fit them into the larger merchandising plans. The vendor then must increasingly depend on the buyer to serve as his communication link with management. Unless he has unusual access to the committee of officials that makes most of the buying decisions, the vendor must rely on the buyer to present his case concisely and effectively in the brief time allotted by busy executives. In any event, the buyer will very probably present the vendor's case much less forcefully than the vendor would himself. A close relationship with the vendor will be of great help to the buyer in selling his decisions to his merchandiser or buying supervisory committee.

Selling to Store Organizations

"More and more buyers really spend more time on sales programs than they do in 'pure' purchasing. . . . Buying power as a brute competitive club has been losing its muscle. Selling power is taking its place."[5]

To be effective, sound buying decisions and programs must still be sold to store managements and their sales personnel. The buyer

[5]Fred Decker, Publisher's View Column, *Marketing Communications,* April 1968.

17

will usually enjoy the services of a highly specialized and skilled staff for matters of display, promotion, and advertising, but he must provide them with their ammunition, and this ammunition will be more powerful if an alert vendor representative has helped to prepare it. There is no better example of the changed and changing role of the buyer than this growing involvement in selling to store management.

Buyer Availability

The busy buyer who insists on punctuality and reliability in matters of scheduling and deliveries should reciprocate by demonstrating strong respect for the vendor's time as well. The buyer should make himself available to the vendor at regular intervals. He should keep in mind that the vendor representative has probably invested much more of his time in the interview than the buyer who is called on.

FACTORS INFLUENCING THE BUYER'S CHOICE OF VENDORS

Almost every day, the buyer interviews representatives of vendors from whom he is not purchasing at present. The vendor representative will put forth as strong a case as possible for his company as an additional source or as a replacement for a present source. The buyer-merchandiser, in turn, must determine how many manufacturers should share in the supply of a category or item, and whether or not to add another source. By spreading his purchases among additional suppliers, the buyer has greater assurance that he is missing nothing that is new and exciting; he prevents supplier complacency and thereby keeps present sources alert and on their toes; he is insured against a decline in competence of a source, possibly through sudden loss of key management; he is better protected against strikes, fires, and acts of God; and he may be in a position to profit from the more advantageous plant locations of a new source.

On the other hand, a decision to take on additional suppliers dilutes the benefits to be gained from concentration on one or a few sources. It lessens the importance of the retailer to the supplier, with consequent loss of trading power in matters of servicing, delivery, and price. It occasionally leads to a wider selection of merchandise at the expense of optimum depth of stocks. It sometimes brings about a sacrifice of quantity discounts and an increase in transportation costs because of smaller shipments. And it increases account-handling costs by necessitating more invoices, more interviews, and more clerical work.

Many of the controlling factors affecting overall buying decisions—the number of items to be purchased and the depth in which they are to be bought—will help to determine the most desirable number of sources as well. Ideal assortment requirements vary among categories. A single source may be most desirable for a standardized, basic line of one outstanding vendor who is providing fine merchandise and service. A famous-brand line of merchandise may be so strongly entrenched and pre-sold by advertising that all other considerations as to number of sources become secondary; customer preference or insistence may dictate that it be stocked. Volatile, short-lived, and high-fashion apparel lines will probably require more sources to ensure that the buyer is tuned in on all alert, imaginative makers. Display space limitation will also influence the number of sources.

After carefully evaluating the many factors, the wise merchandiser will probably strike some sort of middle course. He will secure the advantages of buying concentration by working very closely with one or a very few key resources, but leave the door open to other vendors by purchasing a smaller amount from them. This will encourage the less important sources to strive to improve their positions, and inspire the already important sources to do their utmost to maintain their top spots.

Having determined the optimum *number* of sources from which a merchandise category should be purchased, the buyer must also decide on *which* source to choose in a specific area. Obviously, merchandise salability and price and the vendor's dependability and alertness to new opportunities will be crucial in the selection of a source, as will the cooperation and the servicing provided by the manufacturer in matters of returns, deliveries, packaging, and promotion. The prestige of a supplier or a brand, and its position in the industry, will demand consideration as well. The caliber of a supplier's top management—its ability and depth—should also be weighed when important new connections are being considered.

The buyer contemplating a change of suppliers will, presumably, have found at least equal quality in the possible replacement source. He should also give considerable thought to the prospect of a loss of continuity of supply and service and the resulting temporary dislocations. A long and important relationship, when terminated, may well leave remainders of unbalanced stocks to be disposed of by markdowns and profit losses. However, vendor-buyer relationships can and do deteriorate to the point where severance and replacement are called for. But termination of an important supplier should never be considered lightly, and principals of both parties should meet in an attempt to repair differences before a final separation takes place. Nevertheless, vendors and retailers occasionally grow in different directions; policies change with new managements; new, aggressive companies overtake and outperform some established suppliers. When such changes take place in an industry, buyers must recognize them, weigh them, and react appropriately.

FACTORS INFLUENCING THE VENDOR'S
CHOICE OF RETAIL OUTLETS

The manufacturer of toothpaste, unless it is a special-purpose type restricted to professional dental distribution, will have invested heavily in advertising his product to the general public because of its extremely wide usage and frequent repurchase. He must insure maximum distribution and availability to avoid the costly mistake of pre-selling a product that customers cannot buy very conveniently. No buyer will expect any exclusive privileges in the promotion and sale of such an item, unless it is a very temporary arrangement.

On the other hand, the manufacturer of an item that requires more retailer attention or selling effort will often wish to restrict both the number and the type of outlets in which his product is sold. For instance, it may be decided that customers prefer to shop for the item in a specific type of store, which adds to the image that the manufacturer has carefully created for the product. Thus, expensive perfumes are not likely to be sold in supermarkets. A line of products may be extensive and require considerable investment and display space, forcing the manufacturer to consider credit ratings and the availability of suitable facilities in the outlets he chooses. Electrical appliances, silverware, and cosmetics are examples of such product lines. A manufacturer will not select outlets that cannot give his product the selling effort it requires. And the most desirable retail outlets may insist on some guarantee of exclusiveness in their trading area in exchange for selling and display preference. In short, the most obvious advantages to a manufacturer of restricting his distribution to selected outlets include the opportunity to concentrate the efforts of his selling organization; the tendency of customers to associate exclusiveness with quality and desirability; and the ability to exercise better control over price, stocks on hand, and display when the retailer is encouraged to have a direct interest in the brand or product. Buyers will not only understand the manufacturer's efforts to set up the most efficient distribution pattern for a brand or product; but they will also compete to have their stores as outlets for the most desirable lines.

The ultimate in selective distribution by the manufacturer, of course, is the outright ownership of the stores from which he sells his products. This arrangement puts him squarely in the retailing, as well as in the manufacturing, business. Such complete vertical integration—the control of a product from its production to its sale to the consumer—has been tried with varying degrees of success. Many manufacturers who have been lured into retailing by the natural desire to achieve maximum control of the sales of their products have found that a different set of skills is required from those they possess, and the results of their ventures have, therefore, often been disappointing.

The Franchise

A much more popular method of controlling and guiding distribution by manufacturers is that of franchising. The franchise is a formal agreement in which the vendor offers the retailer such advantages as the right to sell his products within a specific geographical area, cooperative advertising, guarantee of sale, as well as assistance in merchandising and reordering. The manufacturer is willing to take on these expensive functions in order to gain favored positioning of the merchandise in the stores, price maintenance, full-line presentation, support of advertising and promotional programs, and, in general, a type of partnership control in the merchandising of the line.

The buyer must be sufficiently knowledgeable and alert to tie himself and his company only to the best franchisers and to secure the greatest benefits from the terms of the franchise. As both retailers and manufacturers become larger and more sophisticated in their operations, longer-range programming for their mutual benefit will continue to be developed. Franchises clearly fall into the category of important accounts with which the buyer must work closely and cooperatively.

BUYING AND SELLING ETHICS

In addition to his specific purchasing responsibilities, the buyer also carries the burden of maintaining his company's reputation for fair dealing and ethical buying practices. Either by example, oral instruction, or written codes, the buyer will have been impressed with the importance of supporting the image which his management wishes to create and sustain in its industry. The most wanted sources of merchandise can be won over or persuaded to give favored treatment when the buyer handles the account with skill and honesty. Conversely, desirable suppliers can be repelled and lost by blundering or unethical buying practises.

The following considerations are basic to the establishment and maintenance of a good buyer-vendor relationship. The buyer should:

Be open to the offerings of all suppliers; even the most unlikely source should be received courteously for just as long as it takes to determine the value of the offering.

Work hard to establish and maintain a preferred position with the most important resources in each merchandise category.

22

Be as loyal to a good supplier as the supplier is expected to be to the buyer's company.

Never cut off a good supplier without substantial cause, and only after mutual discussion and criticism have failed to produce the desired results.

Make all commitments definite—written, if possible—and require suppliers to be just as precise.

The buyer's relationship with vendors should be marked by mutual respect. He should be fair, friendly, and firm in representing his company. The overly-pliable buyer who inspires the affection of the vendor and cultivates a close, social relationship may find it difficult to represent the best interests of his company at all times.

Practices and Abuses

Both the vendor and the buyer sometimes forget that each is an agent or representative of his company, not a principal. Each carries the good name and reputation of his firm in all his dealings and each should actively promote and defend them. Personal idiosyncrasies that tarnish the image of the manufacturer or the retailer will eventually prove costly and cannot be tolerated for long. When mutual distrust or disrespect is more evident than mutual confidence, the waste of time and energy, and loss of concentration in buying and selling, can be enormous. Suspicion may lead to costly cross-checking, spot audits, laboratory testing, and sampling which distract merchants from their central purpose of promoting sales and profits.

There are certain common trade abuses by vendors against which the alert buyer must protect his company. The buyer must be sure that the vendor is delivering the merchandise bought and nothing else. He must be especially vigilant in those merchandise areas where the products are least standardized, where ingredients may vary, and where hand operations can cause irregular quality (for example, in apparel lines). Substitutions of sizes, styles, and materials can seriously slow down sales and turnover.

The buyer must be able to spot false, misleading statistics and to re-evaluate the occasional vendor who uses them. He must also be on the alert for the commission-compensated, over-loading vendor agent who feels little or no responsibility beyond the order-taking stage of the transaction. He must be sure that the prices, terms, and allowances he is receiving are at least equal to those offered to competitors and other classes of trade.

The vendor and his representative, for their part, should expect and receive comparable treatment. The retailing company interested in building strong, healthy relationships with the best manufacturers will not abuse its great buying powers. Eagerly sought short-term gains should be weighed against long-range consequences and goals. Buying aggressiveness is respected by the vendor as well as by retail management, but, if unrestricted, it can impair or even destroy a valuable relationship. Contracts should be specific and adhered to. Understandings should be written out to avoid later misunderstandings. Cancellations should be by mutual consent, and returns authorized and restricted to specified quantities and items. The buyer should also do his part to see that invoice payment terms are met.

It is sometimes difficult to control or limit the offering by vendors and the acceptance by buyers of gifts, entertainment, and other favors. In extreme cases, these gratuities can be a serious burden to the vendor and an improper influence on the buyer's judgment. Practices within industries vary from extreme permissiveness to extreme strictness, and retail company policies are far from uniform. The undesirability to both retail and vendor managements of having a relationship affected by the giving or withholding of gifts of any kind is evident. Retail management, by example and by frank checkup, should spell out exactly what it considers improper conduct by its buyers. It should be made crystal clear when vendor Christmas gifts, entertainment, opportunities to benefit from stock purchases, and other gratuities are deemed a present or a possible future influence on a buyer's judgment.

No retailer can flourish for long without access to the best sources for all categories of merchandise. Ultimately, after the retailer has supplied the proper settings, it is the merchandise itself that draws and satisfies the customer. This merchandise must come from a

24

supplier who is pleased with the performance of the retail outlet and of the retailer's representative—the buyer.

THE MIDDLEMAN

The manufacturer of a product who chooses not to sell directly to the retailer must employ the services of another to do so. This in-between dealer is called a middleman or wholesaler. The middleman's services may also be in demand by retailers who, for various reasons, are not in a position to deal directly with the manufacturer. In either case, the middleman will charge for his services. The manufacturer will give him a more favorable cost price for the product to pay for his services, and the retailer will pay the middleman a higher price than he would have paid had he bought directly from the manufacturer.

Despite the additional costs, the manufacturer will employ a middleman when he finds it unprofitable to sell directly to small or inconveniently located accounts, or to make a profitable shipment of small orders to small retailers. Retailers seeking the middleman's services are usually small, with limited financial resources and skills. They depend on others to bring together a multitude of varied products for their purchasing convenience.

The Wholesaler. The wholesaler usually stocks a wide variety of staple commodities for the retailer who does not have the sales volume, purchasing capacity, and/or storage space to buy in larger quantities directly from the manufacturer. The manufacturer's high minimum shipment requirements, the increased trans-portation rates on small deliveries and their longer time in transit, are other factors of importance that will make the wholesaler's services attractive.

The Rack Jobber. The rack jobber provides more services than does the wholesaler, for which, of course, he must charge more. He not only stocks the merchandise in his warehouse, but orders it in the proper quantities for the retailer, delivers it, and may price-mark it and decide in what proportion it should be displayed in that category. The retailer pays the rack jobber for the expert handling

25

of a difficult and probably unfamiliar line of merchandise. The "racker" will probably operate the line with less of the retailer's investment because of better stock control, and he will also relieve the merchant of stock-keeping chores and their costs. The buyer must weigh these advantages against the cost of the services and follow up to see that the service is provided according to the agreement.

The Leaseholder. A leased department is run under the store's name by another company. For example, Jones may operate a millinery or shoe repair department in Smith's store under Smith's name, and the buying public will assume it is part of the Smith operation. Jones assumes responsibility for the merchandise investment, the selling costs, and the advertising of the line. Smith, of course, charges Jones rent for space occupied. Prominent categories which lessees commonly operate in mass merchandising outlets are garden supplies, paint, furniture, shoes, records, drapes, floor coverings, hardware, and men's wear.

The Role of the Middleman in Mass Merchandising

It would appear that the larger the retailing chain, the smaller the need for the middleman, and that he could well be bypassed completely. Financial resources are no problem to the mass merchandiser, and his size should permit the employment of specialists with the ability to perform any buying and operating function with skill and economy. Yet the three types of middlemen survive and persist in servicing the largest chains and are actually flourishing in some merchandising areas. If the competent and well-financed buying-merchandising team of a giant retailer can acquire goods at rock-bottom prices and consistently deliver to the stores at a good, competitive cost figure, why does a mass merchandiser turn to a middleman?

Middleman Expertise. A particular wholesaler, rack jobber, or leaseholder may be a superspecialist in a category with unique retailing problems. For example, millinery companies often take over much of the retailer's functions because of their special knowledge of this high-style category, with its exceptionally sharp sales peaks and valleys. Few mass merchandising buyers will have comparable skills in millinery. Wise management, perhaps still smarting from memories of heavy millinery carryovers in other seasons, will provide display space to a specialist and let him do the complete merchandising and stock control job. The buying-merchandising team of the chain will still be responsible for the net productivity of the display space assigned to the milliner, but it will be relieved of the merchandising problems of the selection, reordering, and delivery of this highly volatile category with its very short and sharply-peaked selling season.

Help in Unfamiliar Areas. The mass merchandiser may also welcome the services of a middleman either in an area where he has had little experience, or where the planning of markon, turnover, and/or display is so foreign to the thinking that led to his greatest merchandising successes that he prefers to turn over that part of his operation to someone specializing in it. Some of the largest food chains rely on middlemen to provide such important categories of merchandise as health and beauty aids because their own training and experience involve high-volume, high-turnover, and low-markup categories and they find it difficult to adjust their thinking to the lower volume per item, lower turnover, and higher markup of such lines as toiletries. Or the proprietors of a fast-growing food chain may not want to be diverted by an atypical part of their business at first. However, they may choose to "take it back" from the middleman specialist at a later date, when their organization has matured to the point where the operation of the toiletries department can be absorbed without diverting top management. Wholesalers, rack jobbers, and lessees are well aware of the fact that they are often in the position of teaching chain management their special skills and then being dispensed with by their pupils.

Increased Net Profit, Fewer Risks. Better cost analyses by retailers have also pinpointed where the middleman can be useful. The thinking that relates net profit only to the cost of sales has given way to a more scientific approach to the use of capital funds and to the rate of return on investment. For example, a store that has been buying its own millinery and has achieved a net profit of $1,500 for a particular season may be approached by a millinery specialist who is prepared to lease the same display space and pay a fixed percentage of his sales for the same season, with his total payment coming to $2,500. In addition to the higher net profit, the store's business risk has been reduced in this treacherous category, there has been no merchandise investment, and its customers have probably been made happier by a more skillful operation. It is easy to understand why over 75 percent of all millinery departments in discount chains are leased. Similar successes could be cited for other favorite classifications for leasing such as shoe repair, dry cleaning, groceries in non-foods stores, health and beauty aids in food stores, jewelry, and prescription drug departments.

But leasing also has its liabilities. Store management lacks the control it has over the departments it operates directly. There can be, and are, disagreements over the terms of the lease pertaining to promotion and advertising. Employees may not get along and housekeeping details may be a source of friction. From the standpoint of the lessee, he has "bought" the instant traffic that is generated by the store's reputation and promotion. But he lives in constant fear of takeover by store management whenever it believes it can perform the leaseholder's function more profitably. For this reason, lessees commonly hedge their operations by involving themselves in other businesses or in their own retail outlets.

Return on Investment. The main factor that has led retail chain executives to retain the services of middlemen in so many areas is the rate of return on investment. If a greater return can be had from investment in departments already being operated, or by expansion into other stores, why use capital in areas where leasing is practical? And the shorter-term commitments of leasing permit a flexibility in decision-making that is highly desirable. Merchants vividly recall that gilt-edged investment in ownership of downtown real estate, which produced great rental savings in the 1930's and 1940's, became a heavy burden when shoppers turned to outlying centers in the 1950's. If a store is being operated in a comparatively

28

remote location, far from the company's warehousing facilities and vendors' shipping points, management may prefer to rely more on local or regional wholesalers rather than to invest in increased warehousing or in a local buying staff. Or management may postpone investment in its own warehousing and staff because of temporary conditions in the money market that would make such development very expensive; or a company's rapid growth may have outstripped its ability to build facilities in some areas. Both of these temporary conditions would also lead to the greater use of middlemen wholesalers, jobbers, or lessees.

Customer Convenience. Mass merchandisers find it important to provide one-stop shopping facilities for their customers. The consumer who has a choice between shopping where she can satisfy 70 percent of her needs or 95 percent will naturally prefer the latter. It is important that "outsider" middlemen be used within the mass merchandiser's store, particularly if a much wanted category of service is not offered anywhere else in the shopping center. Jobbers will therefore be given space within a store, or areas may be leased to operators of beauty salons, barber shops, restaurants, snack bars, automotive repair shops, and appliance repair shops. Not only will such service shops contribute to profit through rental payments, but they will also create traffic for the rest of the store and assist in luring the consumer away from another store or shopping area that does not offer as many types of merchandise and service.

The buyer's role is reduced or eliminated where the wholesaler, rack jobber, or lessee functions. However, his expertise in his merchandise category will be important to top management in reaching decisions on when to use the middleman's services. It is anticipated that giant retail organizations, as they mature and acquire greater and broader skills, will take over more of the services now being furnished by wholesalers, rack jobbers, and lessees. But the demise of the middleman has been predicted for years. As long as he can demonstrate and develop the special skills that even the largest retailers cannot duplicate profitably, he will continue to play an important role.

29

2

The Buyer and Store Management

We will not solve our problems by the emotional exercise of the people in selling and operations blaming the clowns in merchandising because they don't provide what the customers want, nor with the people in merchandising blaming the lunkheads in selling for not properly presenting the merchandise, but only, as I have suggested, by management utilization of all the resources of the enterprise toward a common objective.![1]

Nowhere in the distributive process is there a greater need for communication and understanding than in the relationship between the centralized buying-merchandising team and store management. And nowhere is the temptation greater to point critical fingers when either party comes up short of a target.

Somehow, merchandise that had looked so beautiful and salable when presented by a skilled vendor in the buying office has lost some of its luster and desirability in the eyes of store management when first lifted from its plain wrappings without any sales pitch. The buyer focuses his entire attention on a narrow range of merchandise and is seeking the same sort of concentration from store personnel. But store management will have dozens of buyers hoping for the same degree of interest, and must spread its efforts and attention over a much wider area.

[1]Speech by Matt Wigginton, Director of Genesco Inc., at the Southern Retail Institute, New Orleans, Louisiana, February 20, 1968.

30

Chain Store Age conducted a survey of the gripes and peeves of 100 store managers.[2] From the standpoint of the buyer and his role, the results were encouraging. Nowhere on the list did managers specifically mention buying failures as a real problem. But buying divisions play a critical role in helping to relieve many of the store management headaches that were cited, such as building sales, paperwork, inventory and buying allowances. The harassed store manager has a right to expect and receive maximum cooperation from all buying divisions. The individual buyer who helps to smooth the path of store management at every opportunity will be amply rewarded.

THE CASE FOR CENTRALIZED BUYING

No retailer would dispute the obvious advantages of centralized buying to mass merchandising. Yet there is much disagreement as to its limits. Managers of large stores often want more local buying authority than central buying offices are willing to grant. The supporters of centralized buying cite the following advantages:

Specialization of Skills. Capable merchandisers and buyers will possess a knowledge of the market, of the activities of competition, and of the achievements of other stores in the same company that the individual store manager cannot possibly have. Such information is an absolute must today for any retailer hoping to win an edge over his competitors. A central buying operation will also have access, probably under the same roof, to a staff of specialists in promotion, advertising, and display that most separate operations could not maintain.

Lower Merchandise Costs. Larger-scale buying for many stores instead of for one or two will bring lower merchandise costs, more supplier attention, and better service.

Lower Operational Costs. Clearly, one thorough interview between manufacturer and merchandiser for a chain of 100 or more

2 "What Bugs Managers Most," *Chain Store Age,* September 1968, pp. 28-29.

31

stores will be more economical, efficient, and time-conserving than a separate interview with each store manager. Operations will also be less costly and smoother where a central buying office has set up a uniform listing of merchandise by categories, as well as a common procedure for ordering and replenishment.

Uniformity in Company Direction and Merchandising Goals. Top managements of mass-merchandising companies establish clearly defined policies which are part of their operating philosophy and the public image they wish to build. These policies cover pricing, markup, assortments, displays, investment allowances, promotion, and much more. The achievement of company goals would be prevented by wide deviation from these policies by individual stores. Centralized buying is an important arm in the execution of these policies.

Some Leeway for the Store Manager

Obviously, there are certain advantages to giving the individual store manager some latitude in tailoring his assortments and promotions to local conditions. The store manager who is a complete puppet, manipulated by daily directives from central management, is not likely to develop initiative or improve morale in himself or in his organization.

The ideal degree of latitude for store managers will depend on a number of considerations. If the stores are homogeneous, then one merchandising concept may fit all locations without variation. If the chain is a merger of dissimilar operations, on the other hand, the buying must certainly make allowances for local differences.

Since the largest stores presumably have more competent management and are likely to have more capable staffs, size of store will also be a factor in granting buying independence. The buying of basic, staple goods can be more readily automated without sectional variations than the buying of volatile lines like apparel, which have both style and climate peculiarities. The California sportswear market, for example, is so distinctive that buying centered in New York may not fill the needs of West Coast stores. The nature of the individual store's competition may require

32

a considerable degree of authority to make quick, independent judgments. Local shopping center promotions may not fit the scheduled pattern of chain-wide promotions. The competence of the central buying operation is also important in determining the degree of autonomy; some retailers have concentrated on building a strong central merchandising group and others have tended to emphasize local or regional groupings.

In day-to-day operations, the wisest course of action for the buying division would appear to be to do what works: to set guidelines but to be flexible within those guidelines; to be adaptable enough to take full advantage of organizational strength and flair wherever they show up, but to discourage the insignificant, local preferences that distract and sap the strength of centralized, knowledgeable merchandising.

Certain differences in customer preferences and tastes must obviously be catered to. Mittens should not be sent to Miami (but have been), nor sleds to South Texas (it has happened). Smaller sizes are wanted near the Mexican border. Ethnic demands and shopping habits vary within the same city. But the mass merchandiser's low pricing structure depends on large-scale purchasing based on the similarities of demand in his stores rather than on the dissimilarities. Too many variations will dissipate this great advantage he has over the small independent retailer.

A good rule of thumb for the buyer is to fill individual store requests that will permit a profit, as well as some that won't. In other words, unreasonable and unprofitable requests should be granted as far as time and available staff will permit, provided that the effort will encourage initiative, cultivate good feeling, and win store cooperation. The buyer may learn a great deal from the offbeat store manager who offers unusual suggestions or sharp criticisms. Perhaps the buyer has been mistaken in his assumptions about average demand. If the fussy manager requests three times as many yellow in proportion to blue as he had originally received, and twice as many large as small, it may well be that the proportions originally selected by the buyer were out of line for other stores as well. If Dallas is requesting a special type of fashion accessory, perhaps the rest of Texas wants it now too, and the rest of the country very soon.

To avoid the expense of special orders, listing and reordering systems should make proper allowance for significant variances in such local demands as size and color. Profit accrues to the mass merchandiser who distributes large quantities of merchandise economically, with the average locality and customer in mind. The buyer must limit the amount of time he and his staff devote to small, over-specialized requests. But store personnel should know that the buyer recognizes their importance in the selection of assortments, and that he appreciates their value as interpreters of public demand from their sensitive position close to the consumer pulse.

NARROWING THE COMMUNICATIONS GAP

One of the major disadvantages of centralized merchandising is the distance it creates between the buying office and the customer. To do his job well, the buyer must keep up with trends and styles in *his* merchandise categories as reacted to by *his* customers in *his* stores. Central market information may not accurately reflect his particular customers in their particular localities. Without a picture in his mind of his typical customers and without constant feedback which reinforces and adjusts that picture, the buyer is seriously handicapped. In testing new merchandise or fresh promotional concepts, customer reaction must form the basis of his decisions.

Short of spending most of his time in the stores soaking up this information himself, the buyer must depend on store personnel. He must appreciate the importance of a partnership-type, two-way communication with store people, and cultivate it. He must understand that store management faces in a different direction in its outlook and work, and he must adapt the language of his communications to this differing point of view if he is to get through effectively.

The buyer should use every method open to him to narrow the communications gap between him, the store, and its customers. His most vocal critic among store managers may turn out to be his best source of valuable information. Surprisingly, buying errors and misjudgments sometimes remain undiscovered and unreported for long periods of time because of poor communications and lack of teamwork. The buyer should cultivate enough close contacts at the store level to guarantee that customer reactions are getting back to him promptly. He may receive some of his most valuable suggestions and ideas from a salesperson in a store near the buying office. Personnel in competitive stores may be mines of information. Manufacturers' representatives may be very helpful. Written reports on the sale of new and test merchandise may also provide useful tips. All big retailers will have a system for feeding such information back to the buying divisions. For speed, a personal telephone call can't be beat. Memorandums requesting information are cheaper when time is less of a factor. In addition, the buyer should plan to be in the stores as frequently as necessary to learn with his own eyes and ears what is happening to his merchandise selections—how they look on the firing line—and to figure out what he can do to improve their sale. The buyer who, through persistent contacts with store personnel, has achieved a warm partnership relationship, will have acquired a most valuable aid to top performance of his job.

It is not easy to plan and execute a perfect promotion that delivers the right merchandise at the right time in exactly the right quantity for each store, with hard-hitting advertising and in-store display techniques, at just the right price to attract customers and still yield the planned profit. A foul-up in just one of these areas can destroy the effectiveness of a promotion. But the benefits of well-executed promotions are great. In addition to the greater sales and traffic they achieve, success breeds success. Store managements that have consistently reaped the rewards of a successful promotion are more eager to perform the next time. With confidence that a buying division can be depended upon to deliver exciting goods on schedule and with a sound promotional plan, store personnel will follow through in their own self-interest and desire for increased sales. A coordinated sales effort and a healthy relationship with the buying division will inspire store organizations to take greater pains in making the physical changes in display required for the promotion; to use advertising and sign material to better advantage; and to hold back the designated merchandise and not place it on sale until the scheduled date.

↞ THE BUYER AND SHRINKAGE PREVENTION

Shrinkage, or inventory shortage, is the unexplained loss of merchandise between its purchase and sale. It is the measure of profit lost from the disappearance of unsold goods from inventory. Its importance may be judged by the fact that the *Chain Store Age* panel of store managers rated shrinkage second only to personnel problems as the subject that plagues them most.

There is not much that the buyer can contribute to the control of shoplifting except to concentrate on packaging that tends to discourage pilfering. But there is a great deal he can do in other areas. He must buy only from dependable manufacturers who will ship quantities as invoiced, of the quality and in the assortments that were specified. He must also be sure that outer cartons and inner wrappings are of the type and strength to deliver the merchandise to the point of sale without breakage or spoilage. Transportation routings that cause excessive handling or take too much time to deliver perishable, fragile, or seasonal goods are to be avoided. Stores should not be over-burdened with packings that create storage or assembly problems. For example, while working as a store manager, this writer once placed a rather heavy order for toy wagons from a buyer's illustrated listing, which showed the attractive item fully assembled at an excellent profit. In small print under the illustration were the initials "k.d.," which were meaningless to me at that time. I later discovered that "k.d." stood for "knocked down" or unassembled—to save packing and shipping costs. When the cost of assembly and the value of the incomplete items lacking nuts, bolts, and washers had been subtracted, the "excellent" profit had shrunk considerably.

Inaccurate paperwork is another cause of shrinkage in the stores. Items may be counted incorrectly or not counted at all for reorder or inventory purposes. Incoming merchandise may be carelessly counted or inspected. While the buyer cannot control the quality of clerical work at the stores, he can help by running a trim ship himself—by having his assortments properly classified and controlled. His listings of merchandise for reordering purposes should be accurate and up to date. As new items are introduced, he should prune the deadwood that is being replaced. Where possible, he should anticipate the change. Discontinued, slow-moving items encourage shrinkage. The longer an item is in stock, the greater the opportunity for deterioration or disappearance.

The "Coverage Game"

Store managers are under very heavy pressures to control shrinkage in their stores, for their constant vigilance in combating shrinkage is vital to overall management. Since uncontrolled shrinkage can quickly wipe out all net profit, store management salaries and bonuses are usually closely related to success in curtailing these losses.

A manager operating a store whose pilferage rate is much higher than normal must compensate somehow to turn in a reasonable net profit. The most likely and logical way is to raise enough prices to cover the unusual loss: he may increase the prices of selected basic items by 5 percent to 10 percent; he may discount fewer items than other stores; or he may reprice upward some of the new items placed by the buyer.

He also may or may not record the increased prices. In fact, the pressure is very strong for him to "forget" to report that he has raised certain prices; he thereby builds an offset or cushion against shrinkage losses which he cannot anticipate accurately and which may cause him severe financial penalties. His sympathetic supervisors, also striving to keep the shrinkage figure as low as possible, tend to "wink" at the subterfuge and the "coverage game" is on.

What are the likely consequences? In the first place, coverage conceals the true facts. There is much to be said for knowing exactly what the true shrinkage is and how bad it is since covering it up may postpone or even prevent remedial action. The latest reduction of sales and supervisory personnel may be recognized as a false saving if an off-setting increase in shrinkage is pinpointed. If the true facts are not swept under the rug, more security may be employed or some attention may be paid to store layout and fixturing to deter pilferage and merchandise damage. Accountants are vehement in their criticism of this common practice of coverage because of their ingrained faith in accurate figures as a basis for understanding and action.

Unfortunately, like an addiction, the practice of a little coverage is likely to soon get out of hand. If a little of it relieves pressure on the manager, a little more will help even more. Since all managers have shrinkage problems to a degree, all are tempted to follow the successful example of the "cover-upper," and may well be encouraged to do so.

The other danger of the coverage game is its tendency to eventually dominate the pricing of merchandise at the stores—to control the normal considerations of planned markon and turnover. The item prepriced at $1.00 which the buyer had secured at a special low cost and distributed to retail at 77¢ may be offered at that reduced price for a very limited period of time or not at all. Unless the store manager reports the markup, he covers shrinkage with 23¢ each time he sells the item. The carefully laid plans of headquarters, which were based on the retailer's pricing philosophy, overall volume and profit goals, are completely frustrated. The quantity of the item will not sell through at $1.00 as fast as planned, investment will be built up, and turnover lowered—and the buyer probably will never know specifically why.

Admittedly, a manager at the point of sale will see opportunities to increase some prices without slowing sales, and he must be alert to do so. This is especially true of new merchandise whose fresh appeal may have been underestimated by the buyer. But store management should record the increase and inform the buyer of this unanticipated source of profit. Inevitably, when coverage is extensively practiced, it results in independent pricing judgments by local store operations that are hidden from central merchandising divisions and their buyers, thus posing serious barriers to communication and cooperation. The buying-merchandising team, in such cases, may develop its plans without being aware of the crucial fact of actual retail price. Such undisclosed markups will prevent the best-planned promotion of well-bought merchandise from accomplishing its purpose of attracting customers to the stores, and will obstruct the movement of old goods to make way for the new.

Also, unplanned and ill-advised markups are seldom corrected. The addiction to coverage tends to outweigh more rational merchandising considerations. If the marked up merchandise is on hand when physical inventories are taken, the unrecorded extra profit is locked into the system; an item bought to sell for $1.29 but marked up to $1.59, which has not sold out when an inventory is taken, is probably counted at the marked price of $1.59, thereby anticipating extra profit and falsely inflating the value of the inventory.

Perhaps the most serious indictment of the coverage game is that it takes the mass merchandiser's eye off the ball, namely, of selling large quantities of merchandise fast. The manager deeply involved in keeping track of the sum of extra, unrecorded prices in order to keep his shrinkage percentage within his company's specified limits is badly diverted from more important company goals.

The prevalence of coverage, in varying degrees, is high among the chains. Although it is a serious obstacle to the accomplishment of the goals of buyers and merchandisers, they cannot control it. However, they must be aware of it and understand it. And they can minimize it in their departments by giving the stores the average markon they need for profitable operation, as well as the least possible markdowns because of poorly bought or poorly packaged goods.

THE IMPACT OF SELF-SERVICE ON THE
BUYER-STORE MANAGEMENT RELATIONSHIP

In the early days of chain food retailing, the typical customer read from her grocery list and the clerk scurried off to fetch the box of salt, the five pounds of sugar, the three cakes of soap, the can of baking powder—perhaps making a separate trip for each. When the list was completed, the pile in front of the customer was bagged and paid for. Labor was cheap and customers expected complete service.

But as discount stores of all kinds developed, customers came to associate lack of service with price savings, and to accept less service or even self-service. Today's customers are thoroughly trained to serve themselves. They seem to enjoy browsing and setting their own shopping pace. Self-service also tends to encourage the purchase on impulse of items not on the original shopping list.

There are several degrees of self-service. The ultimate, of course, is the vending machine where the customer not only serves herself, but also pays for her purchases without any personal attention from the clerk. The most common form of self-service, however, is unassisted customer purchasing that is paid for at a checkout register operated by an attendant who takes the money and bags the order. An intermediate step between self-service and personal clerk attention is self-selection, where the customer does the selecting but receives or requires the attention of a salesclerk at some stage of the transaction before payment.

The individual buyer will have nothing to do with devising or implementing his company's policies at the point of sale. However, as an agent of these policies, he must thoroughly understand the reasons for self-service and his considerable responsibilities in buying merchandise to be sold under its limitations and opportunities. He must realize that even a slight reduction of everyday selling costs represents a significant economy. In a period of sharply rising labor expenses, the retailer who can control his selling wages and improve his ratio of sales to labor costs has a greater chance to keep his pricing competitive and still make a profit.

Advantages and Disadvantages of Self-Service

Certainly customers have reacted happily to serving themselves in many types of stores. Goods that are attractively packaged, clearly prepriced, displayed by classification for easy location, and readily transferred to a central checkout and payment point have successfully circumvented the heavy costs of personal selling. The customer has not felt deprived of attention and a genuine economy of distribution has been effected by which the consumer profits the most through lower prices.

However, self-service does not always work out as planned.

40

Goods are sometimes unpriced or incorrectly priced. Not all merchandise is or can be designed or packaged to answer all the customer's questions without at least a minimum of personal attention. Store layouts can be confusing or inconsistent. Shopping carts may be unavailable, and central checkouts crowded or undermanned. When selling assistance or advice is sought by customers, personnel may be very hard to locate. Obviously, self-service cannot be absolutely no-service; it must not be translated by customers to mean "come-and-get-it-if-you-can-find-it."

Self-service also severely limits the opportunity to sell many types of merchandise. Higher-priced apparel and cosmetics will thrive when they are sold personally with some degree of skill and knowledge. Multiple and suggestive sales are not encouraged by self-service. The opportunity to trade up customers into better lines is missing unless salespeople are present. Mass merchandisers are constantly weighing the economies of complete self-service against the opportunities that must be forfeited. How much more would be sold if another salesclerk were employed who could maintain complete stocks and display them more attractively? How much pilfering would be deterred if one more employee were stationed in a particular area?

To deal with these problems, retailers may employ more sales personnel in some parts of the store than in others. Although merchandise may be self-selected, salespeople may be within reach to help locate sizes and colors, give opinions, allay doubts, confirm judgments, or handle complaints. Stores may have selling islands or shops with specially assigned clerks and cash registers. Retailers may lease a line of merchandise to a concessionaire who assumes all the selling headaches. But the final arbiter of the retailer's course of action will be the customer: What mixture of expensive personnel and lower prices will most please the most customers and bring the most patronage to the store at costs the merchant can sustain?

The Buyer's Role

To attain maximum volume in his merchandise categories with minimal direct selling costs, the buyer must first of all accept the facts as they exist in the stores. If he works under the illusion that his wares will receive more selling attention than they actually will, he is likely to buy the wrong merchandise in the wrong quantities. The special flair of one manager for selling the buyer's particular categories, or the record of one store with a greater opportunity to perform outstandingly may convince the buyer that all managers and stores can do equally well, and he may overbuy as a result. When the more typical stores do not measure up to the selling performance of the exceptional store, investment piles up, turnover drops, and markdowns loom ahead.

The buyer who understands that he cannot simply dump goods into self-service outlets and expect store management to take the time to plan and execute the complete promotion and sale of the merchandise, will set out to do all he can to pre-sell or help to sell it. The buyer should certainly know more about his merchandise and its salable qualities than anyone else; and he should have learned from experience that it is not enough to simply "build a better mousetrap" and wait for the world to discover it. Among mass merchandisers, more and more buyers and their available staffs have taken on the added function of doing as much of the selling job for store management as they possibly can.

Good packaging is the most obvious key to pre-selling in a self-service environment. If the selling message is so effectively presented by the package that the item attracts the customer and answers all her questions, the costs of personal attention are avoided. If the package is durable and easily handled and displayed, the buyer has helped store management to control damage, spoilage, and profit losses.

Once the buyer has provided a well-packaged item as part of a balanced merchandise selection, with adequate display instructions and a satisfactory replenishment system, he can motivate store personnel to sell more effectively in many ways. Manufacturers' special allowances and free-goods offers, if skillfully presented to store management, offer opportunities for the buyer to win extra selling effort. The support of district and regional store supervisors should also be sought because of their opportunity to encourage selling effort. The sales promotion department may be working on a special plan and may have openings for additional items, which, if promoted, would stimulate store personnel. Vendors frequently distribute brochures or advertising tear sheets that effectively educate and impress store employees on the merits of a line. Such material may be combined with a buyer's letter to store management citing the success of some stores with the line. The buyer who aggressively uses these methods to fight inertia and staleness in the merchandising of his wares will build a contagious interest in and enthusiasm for selling that will reinforce his entire operation.

The bigger and more widespread the company, the greater the problem of communication between store managements and buying divisions. But the need to communicate is critical, and the buying-merchandising team must demonstrate a sincere desire to understand the store manager's problems and to work with him. This is the key to the successful execution of centralized merchandising planning. Without store management cooperation, the best laid plans will founder. With it, possible goals will become certain goals.

3

The Buyer and Merchandise Assortments

Let no young tradesman value himself upon having a very great throng of goods; having just a necessary supply to produce a choice of new and fashionable goods . . . a few goods, and a quick sale, is the beauty of a tradesman's warehouse, or shop either; and 'tis his wisdom to keep himself in that posture that his payments may come in on his front, as fast as they go out in his rear; that he may be able to answer the demands of his merchants or dealers, and, if possible, let no man come twice for his money. . . .[1]

No aspect of retailing is under more constant and close scrutiny than merchandise assortments. How many brands of toothpaste should a merchant offer? How many colors of ladies' sweaters? How many neck and sleeve sizes of men's shirts? Should a food store sell paint? Should a variety store sell groceries? The retailer must not only determine the selection of a particular category of merchandise he will offer his customers, but he must also decide whether or not to offer that category at all. The buyer is often called upon to play a major role in the determination of assortments. It is extremely important, therefore, that he be aware of the nature of the problem and of its several possible solutions.

Many of the commandments that are supposed to govern the

---

[1]Daniel Defoe, *The Complete English Tradesman,* First Edition, 1726.

buyer's determination of assortments seem paradoxical and contradictory. For example:

Keep stocks at a low level—but not too low.
Make stocks keep pace with sales—whether up or down.
Increase turnover—but only at a satisfactory net profit.
Make volume purchases to obtain better prices—but don't overbuy.
Maintain a good assortment of products—but not too many.
Give particular attention to the high-margin inventory items—but don't lose sight of those low-margin products with high turnover rates. [2]

What, then, are the most practical guidelines for a buyer facing a specific assortment problem in one merchandise category? He must, on the one hand, exercise careful control over his selections. On the other hand, he must always relate his buying to the shifting quixotic demands of the customer. Somewhere between these two is the middle ground of sound buying which will yield the most sales at the greatest net profit.

In most situations the buyer will have been assigned the framework for his decisions. He will have been given a dollar investment limit, a turnover goal, and display space restrictions. He will have been well schooled in the image that his company is seeking to build by its choice of merchandise. And even when the buyer is given little final authority in the determination of merchandise assortments, he should be aware of the recurring problems that are behind the decisions made by the policy-making merchandisers and officers of his company. Full appreciation of the reasons behind the formulas given him for merchandise assortments will enhance his understanding and increase his motivation.

ASPECTS OF THE PROBLEM

Obviously, no general merchandise chain store is going to stock ready-to-wear for seven-footers or every shade of thread manufactured. Customers don't expect this. But there exists a large

---

[2] John P. D'Anna, *Inventory and Profit* (New York: American Management Association, 1966), pp. 23-24.

45

grey area where customers are unhappy with the selection they see while retailers maintain they cannot afford to present larger assortments. A merchant's success will depend on his ability to establish a happy medium that will give his customers the choice they want and provide him with maximum sales and maximum profits.

Expansion of Product Lines

The problem of merchandise assortments has been enormously compounded over the last decade by the rapid expansion of product lines. Both manufacturers and retailers have found that the consumer's appetite can be whetted and increased by innovative product design, vigorous promotional campaigns, and attractive displays. Heightened interest in fashion has multiplied sales but has also increased product lines and assortment problems. Product developments in such areas as housewares have opened up new and expanded markets. Kitchen appliances and gadgets have proliferated and the housewife is interested not only in their utility but in their color and general attractiveness as well. A comparison of assortments in today's chain stores with those of ten years ago in such categories as ballpoint pens, candy bars, or ladies' sportswear will reveal the merchant's dilemma. The varieties of color, style, and package size have exploded. The crossroads storekeeper in a remote resort town may still be able to force Colgate toothpaste on a Crest user (or vice versa) in his captive community, but an increasing number of today's more sophisticated customers will seek out those merchants who provide the most appealing assortments.

The Impact of Affluence

The growing affluence of our society has led to the quicker replacement of goods and to an increase in impulse buying. The modern consumer can afford new and attractive variations of a product. Today's homemaker does not wait until her dinnerware breaks to replace it. She has the financial ability to give in to her desire to upgrade the appearance of her dinner table or to satisfy a long-felt wish to own a more elegant second or third set of dishes. In order to successfully exploit this opportunity to sell more din-nerware, the merchant must carefully ponder the extent of the assortment of patterns he will need.

Given their greater financial means, most consumers will yield to the impulse to buy apparel from fashion-right assortments. Here, too, the buying-merchandising team must work hard to provide just the selection to make these sales.

However, if increased assortments have only doubled sales while inventory has multiplied five- or six-fold, profits may not improve at all. In such an event, the merchant's money would be better in-vested in a faster-selling category, in another store location, or even in the savings bank! Executives and financial administrators in companies that develop proper statistical breakdowns will be quick to point out categories with sluggish turnover of stocks. The buyer will be required to release this unproductive investment as fast as possible and with a minimum of markdowns. And, at the same time, he will have acquired a costly but educational experience in assortment management.

Out-of-Stock Conditions

Nothing is more frustrating to a customer or more injurious to a store's competitive reputation than out-of-stock conditions on wanted items. The housewife who has been convinced by expensive advertising and promotion to drive to a particular store to shop for a certain item and doesn't find it there, may be lost forever to better merchants. The store that has determined that an assortment of two articles will get the profitable business and is out of stock on one of them is worse off than the store that has a less restricted assortment.

Most retailers know the old story of the country storekeeper who refused to sell the last piece of any category because he had heard somewhere that an important business guideline is never to run out of anything. This writer is acquainted with a store manager who, knowing that his district manager was coming that day to check the completeness of stocks, prevailed on a customer to accept delivery in the evening of a 10¢ article which was the last one in stock. The district manager departed with a favorable report on stock completeness, and the customer received his purchase as promised.

Diminishing Returns

Writers on the subject of the number of brands, types, or styles of an item that should be stocked repeatedly refer to the premise that 20 percent of the inventory produces 80 percent of the sales and that the other 80 percent therefore produces only 20 percent of sales. Any merchant concerned with the cost of maintaining slower-moving inventory should be much impressed with this statistic, which appeared in an article by John Magee in the *Harvard Business Review.*[3] (See Figure 1.)

This statistic certainly focuses on the expense of maintaining broad assortments, thereby demonstrating the need for buying rules and limits to variety. The aimless drift into meaningless duplication of stock occurs frequently in buying offices that lack clear guidelines and a good understanding of the assortment problem. Mr. Magee explains that "80 percent more inventory is needed in a typical business to fill 95 percent of the customers' orders out of stock than to fill only 80 percent."[4] In other words, an inventory in a merchandise category of $1,000 that is satisfying 80 percent of customers' demands must be increased to $1,800 to meet the demands of 15 percent more of the customers.

It would be helpful to know the number of firms that participated in Mr. Magee's study, as well as the percentage that was involved in retailing. But even if his statistics do not fit the mass-merchandising picture exactly, the concept of diminishing returns as assortments grow is clearly relevant. It is costly to yield to the temptation to carry the inventory necessary to please the last 15 percent of the buying public. The extremely short or tall, or the very fat or thin, are simply unproductive ready-to-wear customers in all but the very biggest mass-merchandising stores. And even if assortments that include these minorities are confined to the largest

[3] John Magee, "The Logistics of Distribution," *Harvard Business Review,* July-August 1960, pp. 89-101.
[4] *Ibid.,* p. 92.

The Buyer and Merchandise Assortments

FIGURE 1

What Fraction of Total Sales Is Accounted for
by What Fraction of Total Items in the Product Line?

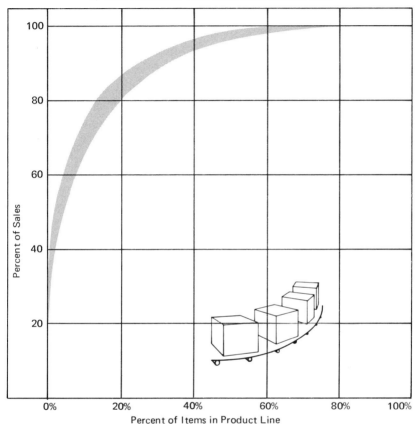

Percent of Items in Product Line

"[This figure] illustrates the impact of small volume items on the cost of operating the distribution system. Yet diversity of product sales is characteristic in American businesses, whether selling in consumer or industrial markets. [The figure above] shows the typical relationship between the number of items sold and the proportion of sales they account for. The figures are based on the records of a number of firms in the consumer and industrial products fields. [The figure] reveals that while 10-20 percent of total items sold characteristically yield 80 percent of the sales, half of the items in the line account for less than 4 percent of the sales. It is the bottom half of the product line that imposes a great deal of difficulty, expense, and investment on the distribution system."

Source: John Magee, "The Logistics of Distribution," *Harvard Business Review, July-August* 1960, p. 91.

49

units of a chain, their share of the buying and administrative expenses goes up because of the smaller volume against which it must be applied. An exact yardstick may not be available for the individual buyer, but he should know that more items usually mean less volume per item and that inventory and handling costs also increase in proportion. The costs of buying a purple sweater that sells ten times as slowly as a pink sweater, plus the money tied up in its slower turnover, plus the larger proportion of rent, heat, light, and other fixed expenses necessarily assigned to it, may make it an unprofitable item to buy in the first place.

A manufacturer or wholesaler of builders' hardware who sells to retailers and builders may be able to reduce his assortments drastically when one item can be substituted for another. Utility is the prime consideration in this case; the elements of fashion, design, and impulse buying are minimal. But most categories are more volatile in nature and the buying-merchandising team must have the assortments to attract a more fickle customer. The particular slice of the buying public serviced by a retailer may have very special social, economic, and ethnic characteristics. Used indiscriminately as a yardstick, the 80-to-20 percent proportion can be very harmful to sales and customer approval.

Diversification—the Six-Syllable Disease

There have been numerous jokes and cartoons about the drug store that was out of aspirin but had plenty of vases, or the hardware store that had cast-iron lawn decorations but no screwdrivers. Diversification has reached ludicrous proportions in some instances: furniture in supermarkets, records in sewing shops, TV sets everywhere. Since there must be a limit to inventory, display space, and time, a store's main categories of merchandise will inevitably be neglected and lose sales when its management becomes involved in too many new, uncharted fields.

Walter Hoving, former president of Lord & Taylor, Bonwit Teller, and later Tiffany, called diversification of assortments a "six-syllable disease." He said that stores are doing "less and less well with more and more departments. They have a little of this and a little of that, and customers end up feeling they don't have

50

anything. They would do better to slough off marginal departments and strengthen assortments. That's the essence of satisfactory retailing."[5]

Rampant diversification inevitably leads to a lamentable lack of depth in the most popular items. Every buying-merchandising team is restricted to some kind of budgeting of inventory funds, and unless total investment is uncontrolled, the money tied up in slow-moving fringe items must be taken from better- and best-selling goods. The result is the frequent depletion of the inventories of the most popular items because they are bought in quantities too small to keep in stock.

One of the most basic tenets of merchandising is to buy and reorder items, sizes, shades, and colors in the proportions in which they sell. Nothing is more fundamental to a successful retail business. And yet, this precept is violated over and over again. Perhaps a buyer with an allotted amount of dollars is torn between adding another item to an assortment or giving depth to the assortment's best sellers. If he yields to the temptation to buy the additional item and leaves his stocks of top-sellers too thin, he has probably made a poor and costly decision.

Not only buyers, but all employees charged with the respon-sibility of reordering at the store and warehouse levels face a similar dilemma. They may have been recently exhorted to keep their total dollar investment down; they may have been advised that they are over-invested at the present time and to "do something about it." What they will do in a high percentage of cases is to replenish the unit that should have received six pieces with two pieces, and all the units that should have been replenished with one or two pieces, if at all, will get their one or two pieces. The temptation is to cut the largest quantities to achieve a reduction of total stocks, and, of course, the largest figures are for the best sellers. Such poor small decisions at this level, multiplied by thousands of items and dozens of stores, can destroy the effectiveness of even the best centralized assortment program, leading to the diversification without depth deplored by Mr. Hoving.

[5]*Grey Matter, Retail Edition,* Grey Advertising Inc., November 1964, p. 2.

SOME SOLUTIONS AND COMPROMISES

Sears, Roebuck grappled with the assortment problem by designating its large, medium, and small outlets as A, B, and C stores respectively. The A stores were huge enough to carry practically everything that the buyers decided to purchase. The C stores, on the other hand, were relieved of the burden of carrying everything by the decision at that time to restrict their selections to hard lines. But the B stores were in trouble; their guidelines were vague and they attempted to carry most of the A stores' assortment in much too limited space.

This unworkable situation was corrected when Sears' management eliminated the classifications of low-volume or low-profit merchandise, thinned down price lines, and established the famous technique of good-better-best buying to designate quality levels. This new approach to assortments settled many problems, particularly as the Sears private brand program developed.

In its largest outlets and even in its vast catalogues, Sears learned that it could not be all things to all people. Other retailers, as well, should recognize that there are certain pitfalls in extension of assortments and in dabbling in peripheral lines. The novelty and excitement of new sources of sales and profits usually wear off quickly, leaving behind increased overhead costs and other headaches.

Choice of Three

It is widely accepted in retailing circles that a "choice of three" in soft lines will satisfy the great majority of customers. That is, experience has shown that a customer presented with three alternatives in the product area within which she is shopping will be satisfied with one of the three and make the purchase. This concept refers to product styles and types rather than to sizes or colors. For example, it could be applied to three types of slipover sweaters which can be substituted for each other in the mind of the customer.

But the application of such a rule of thumb is made difficult by

52

the fact that a particular product category may be a very broad one. Perhaps fashion has brought to sudden popularity a variation of a product, creating the need for an in-depth inventory of at least three more types of sweaters, or a choice of six. Perhaps these newer styles look well on only one age group, making it necessary to continue to stock all other types for the other age groups. Under these circumstances, strict adherence to the choice-of-three concept will lead the customer who is looking for a specific type of sweater to feel that she is getting no choice at all.

On the other hand, there are certain low-volume categories where a choice of even less than three can be afforded. For example, a men's wear department may carry a single style of formal wear to upgrade its total image, though sales and turnover do not warrant stocking even that one.

Buyers for chains of stores of differing sizes and sales volume must vary the extent of their assortments to conform to the physical space available as well as to the type and number of customers. However, a store that is limited by its size and volume may do better to drop a category entirely than to offer inadequate selections that fail to attract customers. So although trial and error by many retailers over the years has indicated that customers are satisfied with a choice of three, such merchandising truisms must be applied flexibly and be tempered by sound judgment.

Sales Surveys

The buyer will be helped in developing his assortments by the sales records of his own group of stores and by the various types of available market information. He will learn to weigh and judge the many, occasionally conflicting, claims and statements of suppliers. He will hear of the successes and failures of competitors and be informed of the latest trends and developments by trade publications. He will take advantage of market surveys on the movement of items in some categories, conducted and prepared by professional teams of market analysts.

In the health and beauty aids field, for example, services may be purchased by retailers or manufacturers which measure actual sales of competitive products by category. A continuing series of counts reveals both the growth or decline of the category, as well as the relative performance of each competitive item in the line. Obviously, such information is most helpful to a supermarket operator in allocating his shelf space and investment.

Among the services available to retailers is the *Towne-Oller Index,* which is widely used by the food industry. This index measures the actual sales and sales rank of each product, and also shows the number of different products needed to meet the demand of a certain percentage of the buying public for that particular category. Suppose, for example, that management has decided to stock all items preferred by 85 percent of its customers in each category of health and beauty aids. The buyer-merchandiser can then consult the *Towne-Oller* current report, which shows how many products combined total up to 85 percent of the market. Based on the data in the *Index,* 20 shampoo items and only four mouthwash items may be required because the fragmented shampoo market presents a different assortment problem than does the more tightly-controlled mouthwash market.

Sales surveys like those included in the *Towne-Oller Index* can be effectively carried out in any merchandise category that is staple enough to make the findings useful. In other words, toy balloons can be measured just as efficiently as shampoos, whereas the short life of the average ladies' sportswear item or piece of jewelry would preclude such periodic analyses of movement. But the high cost of collecting data for these surveys limits their application to categories in which sales volume is large and manufacturers require extremely accurate information on the effectiveness of their advertising appropriations and techniques. For example, a headache remedy manufacturer who is prepared to spend millions in advertising to gain a few more percentage points of his total market must have access to reliable measurements of that market in order to judge how best to reach it. And, certainly, whenever the buyer has such information available to him, his assortment problem is greatly simplified.

In addition to their other virtues, these surveys also serve to illustrate the principle that, for many complicated reasons, customers seem to require more choice in some categories than in others. Perhaps if accurate measurements were available in such areas as home furnishings and apparel, rules of thumb like the "choice of three" would be reconsidered and modified.

Breadth Versus Depth

When the merchandiser has yielded to the temptation to broaden his selections beyond reason, he must reduce his inventory somewhere if he is to secure turnover and hold his total investment under control. By far the most common course of action in such cases is the reduction of depth in assortments, especially of the best-selling selections where there is quantity to be cut.

But one of the greatest strengths of the big chain-store organizations is their reputation for depth in those popular categories for which they have always been known. No variety, food, or drug chain can compete favorably if it is frequently out of stock on the best known brands of say, toothpaste, because it has reduced depth and investment to take a flyer in exotic imported novelties. Standardization of selection has been one of the chief drawing cards of the chains, and to abandon it, even partially, through the addition of other lines is to leave the major part of their customers behind to be gobbled up by competitors. It is interesting to note that the tremendous success in the last decade of the soft-goods self-service stores has been partially attributed to the fact that their assortments have not only taken dead aim at a particular socio-economic level of consumers, but they have also had real depth. The tremendous response of their customers to this combination has resulted in the big retail success story of recent history.

New Products

We have said that the indiscriminate limitation of number of brands or items to fit a rigid formula can be just as disastrous as unlimited selection. Manufacturers of new products are often frustrated by the buying attitude that "you cannot stretch walls." Indeed, many new items are "me-too" copies which vainly hope to capture a fraction of a market and others are undeserving of consumer purchase for any of a number of reasons, but the walls of demand can, in fact, be stretched by innovation, advertising, and other promotional techniques. Today's affluent customer is eager for bright new products. The goal of the buying-merchandising team should be to so manage its allotted inventory dollars that stores are always in-stock on basic popular items and also have available funds to take maximum advantage of new, exciting products and their promotion.

The importance of massive injections of new products into the retailing life line to create growth and excitement can hardly be overestimated. The widely quoted statement by Sears, Roebuck and Company that one half of its sales in 1966 came from products that were not on the market 12 years earlier is startling, but, in fact, such an experience is more typical than unusual in retailing. Supermarkets take on thousands of new products annually and reject even more. Youth is the most avidly new-product oriented group of consumers, and the youth market is both the fastest growing and the most obvious source of future adult sales.

However, a survey that appeared in the March 24, 1969, issue of *Advertising Age* stated that almost 80 percent of 9,450 products introduced in 1968 were considered failures in terms of projected sales goals.[6] The mass-merchandise buyer must decide how to deal with this constant barrage of new products. On the one hand, he would certainly benefit from being among the first to popularize his stores by having a strong in-stock position on a genuinely new, wanted item. On the other hand, he must protect his outlets against product indigestion and over-assortment. How does the buyer know whether a new product really has a new angle that will appeal to and hold a share of the market, or whether it is merely a substitute with no difference except in name?

As a help to the buyer in sorting the wheat from the chaff, the manufacturer will often check the selling effectiveness of his new

[6]Survey by New Products Action Team Inc., *Advertising Age,* March 24, 1969.

product with tests that simulate general market reactions. He will introduce the product into a very limited market—into three widely-separated trading areas, for example—and then carefully measure results as a basis for determining further distribution, changes, or discontinuance. Other manufacturers will test their new products by seeking the cooperation of their favorite retailers. It is to the buyer's advantage to help the vendor in all such testing.

If a buyer is presented with a new product that is ready for national distribution but he himself is still not impressed enough to make a place for it in all his stores, he may try it out in selected stores. If his stores are divided into A, B, and C categories—large, medium, and small—the buyer may test the item in the largest A stores only or just some of the large A stores. Most retailers will have worked out a test and information feedback system that will report on the sale of new items as a basis for further action. Since such test distributions are crucial to the success or failure of a new product, the vendor will wish to monitor the results too, and he will watch eagerly for reorders.

But even the most expert test-marketing is often misleading and the buyer can't possibly try every new product presented. He must frequently exercise his own judgment based on the following considerations:

Uniqueness. Does the product really have something new to offer the consumer? Does it present a totally new market opportunity, or does it vary just enough from an existing product to gain the preference of at least a reasonable share of customers? The survey of the New Products Action Team Inc. gave "vague consumer difference" as the biggest reason for product failure, occurring in 36 percent of the cases. [7]

Quality. Will the product perform well enough to lead the customer to buy it again or to speak well of it to other potential customers? A successful marketing plan that gets the item into the hands of customers can still founder if the product's performance is lacking in any way.

[7] *Ibid.*

Competition. Is the product under the handicap of entering a category already covered by many strong, aggressively promoted items? Do such strong brands and manufacturers already exist that any penetration by a new product would take a long time and be very expensive?

Vendor's Capabilities. Are the manufacturer's promotional campaigns and expenditures adequate? Are his production facilities capable of meeting demand, delivery, and servicing schedules?

Profitability and Packaging. How do the pricing, profitability, and packaging programs of the new product fit the requirements of the retailer? Manufacturers accustomed to selling through wholesalers and small retailers may find it necessary to adapt their programs for mass merchandisers.

The buyer must keep an open mind in the selection of new items, appreciate their importance, and be eager to cooperate when a new product appears to have a chance. But it is also his responsibility to see that his investment and display space in the stores are not swallowed up by the 80 percent of unsuccessful products. Every buyer makes errors in judgment, and he must be quick to review either the rejection or the selection of an item when results prove him wrong.

Seasonal Expansion

"Cherry-picking" is a phrase used by retailers to describe the common practice of merchandising single fad or seasonal items that are not usually stocked and are often far removed from the store's type of merchandise; for example, anti-freeze in drug stores, TV sets in filling stations, and so on. The appeal of such items to the retailer is obvious. With no increase in such expenses as rent, heat, electricity, or personnel, he can get a piece of the sales and profits that someone else is making from these products. In most cases it soon becomes clear that "cherry-picking" sales are minimal, turnover is small, and the total operation of the store is made more complicated. But there are important exceptions, mostly seasonal. Thousands of stores with small or no toy departments from January to November bloom with the Christmas season into very large toy operations. Outdoor furniture becomes important during the summer in outlets that do not carry furniture in the other seasons. Experimentation with these and similar lines will show whether their addition is really profitable after all overhead costs have been properly assigned.

Building on Strength and Eliminating Weaknesses

Sam Neaman, president of McCrory's, in a June 1968 interview with *Chain Store Age*[8] asserted that assortments should not be determined until research has first established where the profits and losses are being made—which departments or categories are carrying the profit load and which are dragging and unprofitable. Once this information has been ascertained, the next step is to build on strength, to increase the selection in the most successful departments. If customers are seeking out a store for its hosiery or cosmetics assortments, for example, these categories should be expanded until their popularity has been fully exploited. A rigid operating formula for assortments should not be allowed to restrict the selection where greater sales and profits are to be had.

Mr. Neaman also objects to the tying up of investment and display space in token assortments of unwanted goods. He recommends elimination of entire profit-losing lines when the buying public has shown that it has no interest in that type of merchandise in that particular store location. Mr. Neaman does not overlook the possibility of nursing back to health some of the sick categories. However, once the rescue attempt has proved unsuccessful, he would be quick to amputate entire lines.

Knowing the Customer

If a store's customers consider its merchandise assortment in a

[8]"Blueprint of a Variety Store, 1970," *Chain Store Age, Variety Store Edition,* June 1968, pp. 37-38.

particular category unsatisfactory, and if there are convenient alternative shopping sources, no amount of theorizing or "logical" explanations will remedy the situation. In such cases, the buying-merchandising team had better get back to the drawing-board quickly.

Assortments should not be strictly dictated to each store and department. The final decision on assortments must be based on the merchant's experience with customer demand in that particular category and geographical area. There must be enough flexibility in the selection offered so that the store or department manager can satisfy his particular slice of the buying public.

THE ROLE OF THE BUYER IN PACKAGING

Buyers and vendors will often collaborate closely in the packaging of products—both in the packaging of the individual item as sold to the consumer and of the cases of merchandise as delivered to the store. However, even when the buyer has absolutely no control or influence over the manufacturer's packaging decisions, he may still act as the consumer's agent by selecting the well-packaged item over the poorly packaged one.

The vital importance of packaging to the successful marketing of any product today can scarcely be overstated. Good packaging not only enhances the product's appeal to the customer and protects its attractiveness and freshness, but also fully adapts to the retailer's display, storage, and transportation needs—an essential requirement in the setting up of effective model stocks. The buyer's role in the actual package design is usually small except where private brands are involved, but his advice may be very helpful to manufacturers. He must be alert and knowledgeable enough to reject, or have changed, any poorly packaged items presented to him.

The value and appeal of a product is heightened by its setting and by packaging that enhances its attractiveness and explains its function. In a very feminine market, packaging may be the deciding factor in customer choice. Gift buying is greatly influenced by the appearance of an item. But even in such basic, unromantic areas as wood screws for home use, both consumers and retailers prefer convenient, self-service, fully-visible packaging over bulk merchandise which requires counting and bagging; and the customer is usually happy to pay the packaging cost differential.

Self-service retailing has had a revolutionary impact on packaging. As sales personnel gradually disappeared from the mass retailing scene, it became necessary for the package to be more easily located and identified by the customer; to sell itself; to answer questions that would formerly have been addressed to the salesperson; to add to the product's natural appeal by its design; and to assure the customer that it would protect the product.

Supermarkets pioneered in self-service and, in cooperation with their suppliers, in the myriad of packaging developments now taken for granted by every shopper. Greater eye appeal, better labeling, better printing, greater product visibility, stronger and lighter containers, better closures, and more sanitary wraps are some of the packaging innovations that can be attributed to the supermarketing industry.

The food industry also led the way in the development of outer containers based on the most economical size for efficient handling, display shelf space, item weight, bulk, and rate of sale. Small, limited-usage items like spices obviously present different outer-container problems from such frequently repurchased bulky items as laundry detergent and paper napkins.

The spread of self-service and mass merchandising to other areas of retailing brought, and still continues to bring, a host of packaging developments. As the retailing revolution continues, so will those responsible for packaging continue to react and adapt. The buyer is not likely to acquire complete packaging know-how, but he must be sufficiently knowledgeable in his own specialized area to exercise reasonable judgment and avoid expensive packaging mistakes.

The buyer will, of course, have a greater voice in the development of private brand packaging for the exclusive use of his company. The major part of private brand packaging will have been worked out by specialists within the company or by outside services, but the buying-merchandising team bears the final responsibility for the success of the package and must make the total packaging evaluation. Has the designer stayed within the boundaries of cost limitations? Have the strongest selling features of the product been properly emphasized, or have some of these features been sacrificed for "prettiness"? The more comprehensive the buyer's knowledge, the greater contribution he will make to the development of successful packages.

Packaging for the Consumer

A recent survey listed 31 pet peeves that housewives have about the packaging of grocery products. The most common complaints were non-spraying aerosol sprays, "tear-heres" that don't tear, leaking liquids, item defects or inferior quality hidden by the packaging, and such "crushees" as cookies in too-fragile packages. [9]

The Packaging Committee of the Association of General Merchandise Chains has issued the *Guide to Better Variety Packaging,* a leaflet with a checklist for better self-selection packaging. It includes the following considerations for the consumer-oriented buyer:

Does package have quick eye-appeal?
Are design, color in keeping with item?
Does package possess individuality?
If part of a line, are packages matched, coordinated?
Is printed matter clear—is lettering uncluttered?
Are all sides used for informative selling?
Does packaging tell clearly what is inside?
If more than one of a kind, is quantity stated?
Is size specified—with age and weight measurements where practicable?
Is kind of material plainly indicated?
Are required government specifications visible?
Are directions for use clear and specific?

[9]*Packaging Digest,* July 1969, p. 5.

Are there instructions for maintenance, laundering, cleaning?
Are there simple, adequate assembly instructions?
Is packaging material the most up-to-date available?
Can customer examine merchandise without tearing package?

This is a thoroughly practical checklist for the buyer. It does not require any great technical knowledge of packaging, but will, if applied, make happier customers—and more popular stores.

Packaging for the Shipper, Warehouseman, and Storekeeper

The well-executed package from the consumer point of view must also have survived the trip from the factory to the store intact, and as economically and conveniently as possible. The Variety Stores Association leaflet also provides the following checklist for the buyer who must meet certain packaging specifications for the sake of the shipper, warehouseman, and storekeeper:

Is size correct for shelf, bin, or on-floor display?
Is package adjustable to both flat and hanging display?
Should package be prepriced by supplier?
Can pricing be done speedily in store?
Will package soil or break easily in stockroom or under counter?
Is there a better material for packaging this merchandise?
Is end-label identifiable in stockroom and on shelf?
For bulky items, is carton with handle feasible?

The manufacturer and buyer who have carefully considered all of these factors will have smoothed the path for those people who must transport the package and handle it at the point of sale, as well as made a substantial contribution to the net profitability of the item.

Optimum Package Size

In many merchandise categories, the most desirable package size will depend on how much the average customer is willing to invest in the item at one time. The trend has been toward the purchase of larger quantities of basic items for convenience and economy. In the 1930's the most popular size of toothpaste in the variety stores was the small 10¢ trial size. In today's more affluent society the family size at about $1.00 sells best, and, therefore, a model stock of toothpaste would include greater quantities of this size. Even with a generous allowance for price inflation, it is clear that the average customer now has the means to maintain larger stocks of basic items at home, and, thereby, to reduce the number of trips she must make to the store.

Manufacturers encourage the sale of larger or multiple units because of the economies derived from larger-scale production. The retailer who sells these larger or multiple units incurs the same overhead costs as with smaller units. The resulting net profits are so much larger that he, like the manufacturer, will urge the consumer to share these greater profits with such offerings as "save 20 percent on the giant size" or "buy two instead of one and save 15 percent."

The buyer, in his crossroads position between the manufacturer and the stores, must be tuned in to all of these packaging needs and opportunities. He need not be a color expert, he need not know the exact bursting strength of containers or the technical descriptions of various polywraps, but he must be able to judge the effectiveness of all packaging in helping to sell more merchandise at a profit. The quality of his relationship with his vendors will certainly influence his success in obtaining packaging that will meet the requirements of his merchandise assortments as well as of his customers.

4

The Buyer and Model Stocks

The primary purpose of any merchandise control system is to have what the customers want with minimal inventories and minimal loss of sales due to stock outs. Effective planning and control of merchandise inventories are the key to overall productivity of a company. . . . Each department must have a merchandise assortment plan geared to each individual store's physical and volume capacities.[1]

A model stock is an exact list of the quantities of each item within a merchandise category that is planned to be in a specified store at a specified time. However, before the buyer can go through the process of setting up his model stocks, the following important matters must be considered and resolved:

The Classification of All Store or Company Merchandise. "A classification has been defined as a segment of customer demand. It is a special kind of segment, however, made up of homogeneous items, reasonably substitutable for one another in the customer's eyes. Bathing suits, thus, can constitute a classification: all suits, allowing for price and size differences, fill the same customer need. Pins, in a notions department, cannot be a classification if hair pins, clothespins, safety pins, and hat pins are all lumped together;

[1]William Levi, Sr., vice president of J. M. Fields, as quoted in *The Discount Merchandisers,* May 1968, p. 74.

65

one type cannot substitute for another in filling a customer need." [2]

The Careful Working Out of a Company Sales Plan as the Buyer's Guide. The buyer may have been an important contributor to this plan by predicting the sales performance of his department.

The Setting Up of Investment Limitations. Disagreements on how much merchandise is needed to "get the business" are as natural as they are endless. The sales-oriented store manager tends to deride strict inventory controls, perhaps quoting the old peddler who said, "You can't do business from an empty wagon." His central office, with overall financial considerations in mind, may, in rebuttal, point out overstocked conditions, questionable ordering judgment in certain categories, failure to clean up slow-sellers in season, and, possibly, the greater success of another store manager who conforms to the investment controls.

The Determination of the Price Lines Within Which the Buying Will Be Done. The spectrum of demand which the buyer must fill will depend on the image that the store's management wishes to implant in the mind of its average customer. This carefully cultivated image may be that of a low-priced, medium-priced, or prestige store, and the buyer must develop his assortments accordingly.

Past records of the buyer's own company and the pricing policies of his most-admired direct competitors will provide a sufficient guide. Very likely, the good-better-best formula will be applied, and it will probably have been found desirable to establish and stick to a limited number of price points. For example, an assortment of ladies' sweaters may be sold at retail for $3.99, $5.99, and $7.99. No doubt many other sweaters were available to the buyer, not only above and below these limits, but within them as well, such as $4.29, $5.49, and $6.88. But merchandisers have learned from experience that the application of the same markon yardstick to

[2]Frank Burnside, "Merchandising by Classification," *The Buyer's Manual* (New York: National Retail Merchants Association, 1966), p. 181.

whatever the cost is, and the resulting unlimited number of price points, complicates the mechanics of setting up and adjusting model stocks, and of display, promotion, and advertising. Most important, it confuses the customer and distracts her from the more important factors of style, color, and size. Most customers have a general price range in mind when they approach an assortment of a category and a 5 or 7 percent difference in price is of little consequence to them. Moreover, if the sweater assortment follows a single price line its style range will be more impressive than if each sweater has to be examined and considered separately as to price.

But the buyer must not assume that his present price-lining policy is infallible. In setting up his assortments he must be quick to note if an important segment of his customers is not being properly served. Perhaps the price points are too far apart, or perhaps the lowest point is not low enough. If the competition has recently sharpened its pricing in the lowest range, perhaps the buyer ought to take similar action. If the general price level is moving up or down, the buyer must protect sales and profits by appropriate action. And in order to permit profitable entry into new areas, the buyer must always be looking for merchandise in higher price ranges than those he already carries.

The Thorough Screening of All Suppliers in the Market for Comparative Dependability and Skill. Each supplier will probably have an established track record as to maintenance of quality, fashion rightness, packaging, delivery reliability, and promotional abilities. Any one of these factors may be conclusive in the final choice of items for the model stock.

The Establishment of the Amount of Display Space in the Store or Stores as well as the Location of the Space. Physical space limitations are especially important when bulky items are being considered. It may be necessary to sell from samples only in some cases. Store location in prestige or budget areas will also be a factor.

* * *

Once these matters have been resolved, the buying merchandising team will proceed to establish model stocks of appropriate depth and breadth. Obviously, a poor job in the setting
up of model stocks will be crippling to any merchandise operation.
While corrections in model stocks of basic merchandise can be
made rather quickly, whole seasons can be lost in fashion merchandise if opening stocks are wrong. At this point, the buyer
becomes a central, crucial figure who has a vital contribution to
make to the success of the entire operation.

A MODEL STOCK OF TOOTHPASTE

Suppose a buyer has been given expected sales and turnover
goals for toothpaste and has been asked to set up a model stock for
the largest size store of three classes of outlets described as large,
medium, and small. Toothpaste sales are $100 weekly and four
weeks' turnover is sought at store level. Planned total stock of
toothpaste on hand, then, is $400 at retail price for this particular
store (four weeks times $100 weekly sales). Now decisions must be
made on brand, size of package, and depth of stock by item.

Brand. Statistics on brand preference are available from several
sources: intra-company figures, which will show present as well as
past sales by brands (a little investigation into past figures will
indicate any trends away from one brand and toward another); the
buyer's regular contacts with vendor representatives, which will
have kept him up to date on recent and projected developments
that might affect his decisions, such as new products, new sizes, or
new promotions; and highly sophisticated surveys from several
skilled companies that specialize in sampling product movement at
the point of sale. (The considerable cost of these surveys is worthwhile because the stakes are high. The market is huge and high
advertising costs require taking careful aim at a known target—and
not missing by very much. But the buyer must understand how the
various surveys are constructed and what they actually measure in
order to sift conflicting claims.)

Armed with this background information, the buyer considers, say, ten brands of toothpaste: A,B,C,D,E,F,G,H,I, and J. Assuming that Brand A outsells Brand J, the slowest-seller, by 20 to one, it is immediately apparent that spreading a $400 investment over ten brands would allow no concentration on the best-selling Brand A. For example, suppose that a minimum investment in J, because of packing sizes, is $15. Then Brand A should have 20 times as much investment in the model stock, or $300. This would leave only $85 from the $400 to be shared by the other eight brands that sell better than J, and they would be badly shortchanged. Obviously, Brand J does not belong in the model stock of our mythical store. But how about Brands F,G,H, and I?

Remember now that all incoming information to the buyer has been sifted and evaluated. Such influences as new products, advertising campaigns, geographical and ethnic preferences have already been weighed. It is further assumed for this example that all relationships with vendors are excellent and that none of the brands has an edge in such areas as discounts and delivery costs.

The high cost of maintaining inventory aimed at the purchasing preferences of only 10 to 15 percent of customers has already been noted (see Chapter 3). And since brand preference is not necessarily brand insistence, the shopper who would normally choose Brand J has probably been conditioned by lack of availability to accept Brand A or B fairly happily—perhaps just as happily. Thus, a selection aimed at 85 percent of customer preference would surely satisfy 90 percent very well, and would probably meet 95 percent of the demand without loss of sales.

Fortunately, for buyers of such health and beauty aids as toothpaste, studies like the *Towne-Oller Index* are available which measure the number of toothpaste items that total any given percentage of sales. It is therefore possible in this particular category to establish a model toothpaste stock consisting of all items in the *Index* in the desired 85 percent range.

Suppose, then, that we set our limit at 85 percent of customer sales and find that it eliminates Brands G, H, I, and J, which, when combined, represent only 15 percent of sales and will therefore be excluded from our model stock. Now we have six brands (A,B,C,

D,E, and F) to stock and $400 to spend for them. Investment by brand then comes out as follows:

Brands	Percentage of Market	Percentage of Our Inventory After Brands G, H, I, J Have Been Eliminated	Dollars of Inventory at Retail Value
A	25.0%	29.5%	$118.00
B	16.0	18.8	75.00
C	15.0	17.5	70.00
D	11.0	13.0	52.00
E	10.0	11.7	47.00
F	8.0	9.5	38.00
	85.0%	100.0%	$400.00
G	7.0	—	—
H	4.0	—	—
I	2.0	—	—
J	2.0	—	—
	100.0%	100.0%	$400.00

Figure 1 shows not only our six selected brands in graphic proportions, but also the four rejected brands and their 15 percent of the market which it has been decided it would be unprofitable to cover.

Size of Package and Depth of Stock by Item. Assume Brand A is manufactured in four sizes and we have $118 to divide up among them. At this point, it is a good idea to consult whatever statistics are available on movement by size. Most mass merchandisers will have their own records of purchases by items, and vendors will be happy to supply their figures. Suppose this investigation shows the following:

Retail Price by Size	Percent of Volume by Size	Converted to Dollars	Converted to Dozens*	Actual Dollars
$1.00	50%	$ 59.00	5 Dz.	$ 60.00
0.75	15	17.70	2	18.00
0.50	15	17.70	3	18.00
0.30	20	23.60	6	21.60
		$118.00		$117.60

* Rounded off to conform as closely as possible to assumed standard packing of one dozen to avoid the costs of breaking up full packages.

The Buyer and Model Stocks

FIGURE 1 Sales Volume of the Ten Best-Selling Toothpastes

Brand A 25%*	$118+
Brand B 16%†	$75
Brand C 15%	$70
Brand D 11%	$52
Brand E 10%	$47 85 Percent of Market
Brand F 8%	$38
Brand G 7%	
Brand H 4%	
Brand I 2%	15 Percent of Market
Brand J 2%	

*Percentage share of market by brand.
†Proportion of $400 model stock invested in brand.

71

Our model stock for Brand A is shown in the fourth column. This procedure will work well for Brands B, C, and D also, but E and F present a slight complication. Figure 1 shows that they deserve $47 and $38 of our model investment respectively. Dividing up Brand F's $38 into four sizes as we did with Brand A gives us the following:

Retail Price by Size	Percent of Volume by Size	Converted to Dollars	Converted to Dozens	Actual Dollars
$1.00	50%	$19.00	1-1/2	$18.00
0.75	15	5.70	2/3	6.00
0.50	15	5.70	1	6.00
0.30	20	7.60	2	7.20
		$38.00		$37.20

But quantities in the fourth column for two of the four sizes do not conform to our one dozen standard pack. The logical decision here would be to drop the 75¢ size and to add the available dollars to the best-selling $1.00 size to bring that quantity up to two dozen.

This example of setting up a model stock for toothpaste is about as simple as could be contrived and one that enjoys maximum help from available statistics. There is very little buying skill evident in the decisions reached. It presents more of an arithmetical or minor engineering problem.

Complicating the Problem

Some of the factors that we have omitted from consideration to avoid complications include the following:

Heterogeneous Categories. Toothpaste, like many other merchandise categories, is not strictly homogeneous. For example, if Brands E, F, or G contained fluorides and the others did not, perhaps the buyer should list one of them in preference to non-fluoride Brand D because fluoride-users may insist on this ingredient whereas other brands might be more interchangeable. A brand might also be purchased because of special preference by children or denture wearers.

Discounting Policies. Perhaps the company's discounting policy ought to be considered. If the best-selling larger size is going to be heavily discounted, what will be the impact on its sale and on the sale of the next un-discounted size?

Promotions. Any long-range TV or other promotional programs might conceivably change brand share-of-market percentages in the next several months.

Profit Margins. The largest size of toothpaste is commonly reduced sharply in price or even sold at a loss as a "loss leader." Most classes of retail trade respond in varying degrees to maintain a competitive image. Smaller sizes are less likely to be price-cut and, therefore, carry more profit percentage. To what extent, then, should profit margin by item be considered?

Display Space. Fewer items require less display space. This is much more of a factor when bulkier items than toothpaste are involved, but smaller stores will appreciate having fewer items in any category if the same dollar volume can be had.

Customer Satisfaction. The intangible factor of customer selection satisfaction must be weighed. At what point is the consumer going to feel that she is being offered a good selection of toothpaste (type, brand, and size; pricing is a separate problem)? Although all merchants will surely stock Brand A in the best-selling size at a competitive price, how can they be sure that the consumer will still prefer to buy this one item where many other brands and sizes are offered, rather than where her favorite is the only one available? No statistic or index can measure this.

Overhead Costs. Buyer-merchandisers know that concentration by brand and item reduces overhead in many small ways—fewer printed entries on forms, fewer items to count and reorder, fewer vendors to deal with and make payments to. But, again, at what point does concentration leave the consumer sufficiently unsatisfied that she will prefer to do her shopping elsewhere?

* * *

Thus, below the surface of decision-making in even the simplest of categories, complications abound. Even in this relatively staple and stable area, with ample statistical guidelines, good buying goes far beyond arithmetic in setting up model stocks.

A MODEL STOCK OF A HOUSEHOLD CATEGORY

Let us consider a model stock of kitchen container ensembles—that is, canister sets, bread boxes, waste baskets, and so on, in matched sets. Assume, again, $100 weekly sales but a six weeks' turnover period this time, and, therefore, a $600 model stock at retail ($100 sales times six weeks).

In setting up our toothpaste model stock, we consider brand, package size, and depth of stock by item. In this category, however we are confronted with the additional problems of quality, design, and color, and we are now dealing with bulky merchandise which requires greater consideration of the available display space. Moreover, the sophisticated sales surveys that were consulted for the toothpaste model stock are not available for housewares.

To reduce the problem to manageable proportions, let us handle the category in units of sets. For instance, the buyer knows (or the information is readily available to him) how many canisters are generally sold in proportion to waste baskets and bread boxes. We shall presume that this proportion is uniform among all sets and shall arbitrarily establish a retail price of $20 as the value of a typical complete set of the middle, best-selling type. With $600 to invest, this shapes up our problem to the purchase of 30 sets if all retail at the $20 level. But we have not dealt with the problems of price lines (quality), display, pattern, and design.

Price Lines. In deciding on price lines and, therefore, on quality, we will assume from buying experience, company records, competitors' selections, and information from vendors that the average of $20 per set breaks down into three ranges of good-better-best at $16, $24, and $30 per set. Suppose we also have the information

74

that our sales volume is anticipated to be divided among the three ranges as 45 percent, 30 percent, and 25 percent respectively. Applied to our allotment of $600 retail dollars, this works out as follows:

Range	Percentage of Retail	Model Stock Retail Dollars	Retail Price per Set	Number of Sets in Model Stock
Good	45%	$272	$16	17
Better	30	192	24	8
Best	25	150	30	5
	100%	$600 (approximately)		

Display Space. The store operations division and/or the display division will have decreed roughly or in great detail the square feet of display space available to the buyer. This allocation will have been carefully worked out from the proportionate contribution the buyer's kitchen ensemble category makes to the store's total performance. Yardsticks of sales and profit in relation to the space occupied will have been applied. In all probability, the type of display fixtures will also have been determined. Perhaps actual experience will have shown that an assortment of six different sets can be displayed attractively in the assigned space, and nine sets if crowded.

Pattern and Design. In most categories of merchandise, there is a standout best-seller, whether basic like our Brand A toothpaste, or a "far-out" ladies' sportswear item. Reams have been written and hundreds of speeches made on the need to promote, display, and invest most heavily in the best-selling item, size, color, or pattern. Assuming that a red plaid design has been rolling up 35 to 40 percent of sales and is still going strong, we will invest 40 percent in this top item, or 12 of our total 30 sets, and call it Item A.

The final resolution of our model stock problem now depends on intuition and supposition. We know the following:

Sales ratio by the three price lines—good, 45 percent; better, 30 percent; and best, 25 percent.

Sales ratio by pattern and color, determined from sales records and

trade sources—40 percent investment in Item A.
Display space limitations—6 to 9 different sets.
Total number of all sets we may stock—30.

The model stock, as finally determined by the buyer after he completes his evaluation of all the above data, is assumed to be:

Pattern/Color/Design	Allocation by Sales Ratio and Retail Price per Unit			Total Dollars at Retail
	45%	30%	25%	
	$16	$24	$30	
A	9 sets	—	3 sets	$234
B	—	6 sets	2 sets	204
C	5 sets	—	—	80
D	3 sets	—	—	48
E	—	2 sets	—	48
Totals	17 sets	8 sets	5 sets	$614

Some of these final determinations are necessarily arbitrary because the example is not large and we cannot deal with fractions of sets. Conversion of retail price ranges from percentages of sales to actual number of sets in the model stock gives us 17, 8, and 5 sets in our good-better-best setup. Multiplied by their retail prices, the three ranges come to 45 percent, 31 percent, and 24 percent compared with out model of 45 percent, 30 percent, and 25 percent. The total dollars at retail is $614 compared with our model of $600. We met our display limitations of six to nine different sets by choosing seven.

Complicating the Problem

Certain complications in our housewares model stock problem are beyond the help of statistics. Many factors in addition to the ones considered above may also influence the buyer, including the following:

Color. Suppose the color black in kitchen decor is developing strength in large cities only. *Decision:* Strike it off the model stock but make it available to selected large city stores by some sort of special listing.

New Developments. Vendor Smith & Jones uses a new type, shape, or material on his canisters which will probably increase the popularity of Item D. *Decision:* Upgrade this item's importance in the model stock.

New Opportunities. A merchandising vice president, on the basis of a communication from store management, has recently reported an opportunity for more trade-up—that is, the chance to sell higher-priced items in kitchen decor articles. *Decision:* Give greater emphasis to the "best" $30 price line (or possibly test an even higher price line).

Local Preferences. The store operations district supervisor reports that in the southwest most customers want only red and green kitchen accents and that assortments and model stocks should have more of these colors and less of the others. *Decision:* If investigation of other sources of information supports this report, advise stores in this area to substitute alternate items in red and green for some of those in the all-store model stock, and provide these stores with the necessary supplementary information or listings to do so.

Trends. Home decorations experts and manufacturers are touting a ceramics look as the next vogue in kitchen decor. Department and specialty stores are already showing it. *Decision:* The buyer's experiences with the rate of development of such trends and the lag in demand between specialty and mass-merchandise outlets will guide him in the determination of the timing of his initial investment and its extent.

Private Brand. The company is large enough to have a private brand in this category, and, therefore, at least one exclusive pattern. *Decision:* Give special preference to the company brand in the plan.

Profit Margins. Profit margins will be more of a factor in this merchandise category than in toothpaste, where there was considerable uniformity. *Decision:* Profit may be decisive in the selection or rejection of sets. The more heavily advertised lines commonly give less percentage of profit to the retailer because a demand or preference for the item has presumably already been established through advertising or other manufacturer efforts which obviates some promotional and selling expenses by the retailer. The buyer must judge how strong a brand preference has been built by the advertising and how much profit he can give up to gain its advantages.

Freight Costs. Freight and space rental costs that increase with weight and bulk must be given more attention in this category than in categories composed of smaller items. *Decision:* Consider concentration of purchases with fewer vendors. Check plant locations and shipping points more closely for possible freight cost savings. Check suppliers for those with the best records for reliable deliveries. A carefully-conceived model stock plan can be a buyer's nightmare without delivery of merchandise on schedule.

Varying Demand Patterns. Demand patterns in kitchen decor may vary both geographically and by type of household—for example, apartment dwellers may have different preferences from people who live in rural areas. *Decision:* Add flexibility to the model stock plan by providing alternate item listings to satisfy these differing demands, but be sure the demand sought in this way is substantial and that it does not represent merely the small percentage of customers who cannot be served profitably.

Untested Items. Perhaps one or two of the ensembles are so new or so radically different that no selling history is available and manufacturers' claims are conflicting or their enthusiasms are suspect. *Decision:* Consult the fashion coordinators, shoppers, or other knowledgeable people whose services might be available and whose judgment has already proved helpful. Occasionally, sound objective evaluations will come from clerks or stenographers who are typical homemakers. If the buyer is a man and the category is usually purchased by women, he should give great weight to female judgment.

These complications have been cited to make our example more realistic. Such problems dominate the final determination of model stocks after the statistics have gone as far as they can. If the buyer's private consultants (the secretaries, clerks, and so on) unanimously agree that an untested item is simply "much prettier," then all judgments based on more conventional and statistical considerations had better be revised. A great percentage of the exciting new merchandise developments come from such intuitive, inspirational, non-scientific sources. The buyer with the necessary enthusiasm and natural flair for his role will develop these intuitions himself and thereby become an important contributor to his company's total performance.

A MODEL STOCK OF APPAREL

We now enter a quite different merchandising area—the world of fashion and wearing apparel—almost 100 percent non-staple. This is an area in which historical data, except for size ratios, are comparatively useless.

The approach to a model stock in a fashion category is similar to that for toothpaste and kitchen ensembles up to a point. As in other categories dollar and display limitations will have been determined on the basis of expected sales and turnover.[3] Seasonal characteristics will also have been provided for by increasing the category's dollar allowance in advance of its peak selling season and reducing it or eliminating it entirely in advance of its slow selling season.

Our immediate concern involves a model stock of ladies' sweaters with which to open the season in the same mythical store that has

[3]This is not automatically the case. A buyer may be able to convince his superiors that a surprise development or unusual growth in a category warrants extra attention and investment dollars.

just settled its toothpaste and housewares problems. We shall assume a retail dollar limitation of $500, good-better-best price lines of $3.99, $5.99, and $7.99, and an estimated volume of 40 percent, 30 percent, and 30 percent, or $200, $150, and $150. It is further known that four sizes fit over 85 percent of the customers and that these sell at the rate of Size A, 20 percent; Size B, 30 percent; Size C, 30 percent; and Size D, 20 percent. Our model stock then shapes up this way:

Retail Price	$ 3.99	$ 5.99	$ 7.99
Estimated Percentage of Sales at Retail	40%	30%	30%
Applied to $500 Investment	$200	$150	$150
Converted to Units	50 only	25 only	19 only
Units by Size			
Size A (20%)	10 only	5 only	4 only
Size B (30%)	15 only	8 only	6 only
Size C (30%)	15 only	7 only	6 only
Size D (20%)	10 only	5 only	3 only

Complicating the Problem

The factors that complicated the buying of staple, basic merchandise will also have their effect here, but the guidelines are much more volatile. Fashion merchandise has its own special set of problems. No amount of investigation can reveal for sure the strength or longevity of a fashion trend. Quick changes make quick decisions vital. Faster and more expensive transportation routings are probably needed. Because demand is less dependable, pricing may require a higher original markon to offset later markdowns in order to average out at the planned markon. For example, a group of high fashion sweaters purchased to sell at an average retail price of $8.00, may first be priced at $9.00 to allow for end-of-season clearance at $7.00, so that the planned average price of $8.00 may be achieved. Flexibility and timing become all-important and the makeup of the 50 sweater assortment at $3.99 will certainly change during the season.

The fashion buyer will be operating on an overall merchandising plan conceived by top management. This plan will have been carefully broken down by merchandise classification and category. Allowed dollars of inventory and the planned profit will have been assigned. But mathematics are less helpful here than in other categories and may even be misleading. Bold, quick action is needed not only in the setting up of opening stocks, but also in the replenishment of store stocks to reflect fashion trends and shifts in demand.

MODEL PROFITS

A critically important element of retailing, of course, is the profit margin—the difference between what the buyer pays for an item and what it is sold for to the store's customer. Profit goals will surely be given to the buyer to work with, along with the expected dollar sales, turnover figures, and dollar investment figures. The composition of a model stock of a category of merchandise will be considerably influenced by the profit goal for that category—how much cut-price promotion is expected in one particular price line or in all, and how competitive management feels it must be in its pricing.

The final planned profit percentage figure may be hotly disputed. Buyers and their merchandising supervisors commonly agree that they could greatly increase their sales and profit dollars if they were required to maintain a smaller profit percentage figure. For example, the buyer may be told to average out his merchandise profit on ladies' sweaters at 45 percent. However, he may believe that an average profit of 40 percent would enable him to price the sweaters so much more attractively that he would sell more than enough to make up the difference in percentage profit between 40 and 45 percent, and end up with even more profit dollars. But he may be turned back by his superiors and ordered to trade more sharply for values that will yield both the dollars *and* the planned percentage. Too high a profit margin reduces the sales volume on an item, but too low a price can result in great sales activity without profit.

The company's discounting policy will, of course, determine the profit margin in many categories. Toothpaste is frequently used as a promotional leader or traffic-builder at markons from zero to 10 percent. Because of its universal usage and frequent repurchase by the average customer, it is an ideal item with which to attract shoppers to the store and build an image of savings and value. But other retailers, like the corner druggist whose image is more likely to be based on professional service or convenience, will choose to operate on a smaller toothpaste volume at a 25 to 33 percent profit margin. The buyer may have some influence in determining the profit margin in this area but, in general, he will be working within the framework of his company's overall discounting and general pricing policy.

Company executives faced with choices like that of operating with a 10 or 33 percent profit margin in important volume categories need all available information to guide them. Variations in pricing policies among companies or among categories within the same company point up the importance of measuring the profitability of individual items. Sales figures are rather meaningless unless we know that the sales are made at a profit; and profit percentages don't mean much unless the sales volume to which they are applied is satisfactory. The best combination of retail sales and profit percentage will yield the maximum profit dollars, and profit dollars are the true measure of successful merchandising. It might, for example, be found that dollar profit production of a big category is extremely low in relation to investment and display space, even after a generous allowance has been made for its advertising and traffic-building value.

In a study made in retail food stores, "direct product profit" was measured for individual items. These figures were built up to profit figures by product categories, which became the basic tool for experiments in product assortment changes for greater profit, as well as in pricing and space allocation changes for better profit balance.[4] For example, assume that a food chain conducted such

[4] Robert D. Buzzell, Walter J. Salmon, and Richard F. Vancil, *Product Profitability Measurement and Merchandising Decisions: A Pilot Study in Retail Food Stores* (Cambridge, Mass.: Harvard Business School, 1965).

an analysis of the profitability of its baby food category. Dollar profit figures by item show that competitive pricing had driven the profit dollars on baby fruits in the small size jar to such a low point that the huge volume of sales still left them far below the average profitability of the department in relation to space occupied and dollars invested. Corrective action might have been delayed indefinitely if dollar profit figures by item had not been available. It is predictable that, in the future, retail management will speak more and more in terms of profit dollars rather than in terms of their separate ingredients—sales and profit percentages.

5

The Buyer and Merchandise Replenishment

Merchandise control is a tool designed to implement the main-tenance of ideal assortments. It is a system of recording and reporting quantities on hand and on order of individual items, and their respective rates of sale. . . . Stock controls cost money. But the true cost of operating without scientific merchandise control may well be more than the expense attributable to stock control on the operating statement.[1]

Merchandise that is bought in the right mix of prices, sizes, types, and colors, attractively displayed, and aggressively promoted, will surely sell. As the merchandise is sold, the stocks become depleted and must be replenished quickly and economically. The determination and maintenance of inventory are the two essential ingredients of merchandise or stock control.

The crossroads candy store proprietor who is running low on bubble gum is likely to have a hit-or-miss system of replacement, or to rely on the periodic visits of a jobber representative. The small drug store operator will probably replace his cough medicines and his analgesics piece by piece via daily telephone calls to his wholesaler, who must deliver these small orders very frequently. These time-consuming services are reflected in the higher prices

[1]Edwin L. Harling, "The Theory of Merchandise Control," *The Buyer's Manual, op. cit.,* pp. 150-151.

that both the retailer and customer must pay for the merchandise. Obviously, the mass merchandiser who buys infinitely larger quantities has a greater opportunity to sell at lower prices and to profit through better stock replenishment techniques.

COUNT AND RECOUNT

The most primitive form of merchandise replenishment is the count and recount method. The procedure is simply to count the quantity of the item on hand, add to it any quantity previously ordered but not yet received, subtract this total from the last previous count to determine sales, and then decide on the additional quantity needed, if any. For example, suppose a hardware retailer is considering replenishing his stock of a particular type of screwdriver. He counts two on hand and finds from his records that he had ordered six more a month ago. He then subtracts this total of eight pieces on hand and on order from the total of his last previous count, which his records show to be 15 pieces, and determines that he had sold seven screwdrivers since his last order. Finally, he decides that if he is selling screwdrivers at the rate of seven a month, and has eight pieces on hand and on order, he should reorder another seven for the upcoming month.

Count and recount can be as simple as the thought process that every housewife goes through in restocking her kitchen shelves, but it can also have many refinements and variations. The housewife will know from experience how much her family uses of such staples as sugar and milk. She will base her purchase quantities on the time interval between shopping trips, or possibly on how much cash is available until next payday. On the other hand, the mass merchandiser will have carefully calculated model stock quantities for his basic items. He will have determined reordering formulas based on a planned turnover, ordering intervals, and replenishment time. All of these factors will have received considerable top management study with regard to clerical costs, the time required for an order to reach the supplier, the time needed to produce and ship the merchandise, time in transit, seasonal variations, and safety factors.

Count and recount can be highly effective in skilled hands. Consecutive counts provide a running record which reveals average sales, peak sales, and trends up and down. In the replenishment of the more volatile fashion goods, it is necessary to point out the winners and losers quickly and accurately; count and recount on a weekly or even more frequent basis will accomplish this effectively. Because of its comparatively high cost in time, however, this method of stock maintenance is likely to be confined by mass merchandisers to higher-priced items where its percentage cost would be lower.

THE EYEBALL CHECK

An important short-cut alternative to count and recount is the eyeball check. In this procedure, the checker does not actually count the item. Instead, he or she observes the degree of "emptiness" of a specific display space. For example, assume that a display shelf space in a supermarket or variety store has been assigned to hold 36 pieces of the large size of Brand X shampoo. The reorder clerk will have been instructed to observe whether or not the space has been depleted by sales to the point where another carton of the item can be fitted in. Suppose the carton contains 18 pieces and observation quickly indicates that there is, in fact, space for another 18 pieces. Without actually counting to determine whether or not the stock in the space has been depleted by exactly 18 pieces, the clerk enters a check mark, or the quantity 18, on the reorder form and passes on to the next item. More simply, if there is space for another full container of the item, it is ordered; if there is not, it will not be reordered at that particular time.

Obviously, considerable clerical time is saved by the eyeball check over the count and recount method. But a great deal of planning has taken place to make this economy of time possible. First, records will have been consulted on the sales of the large size of Brand X shampoo in relation to competing brands and sizes, and space assigned accordingly. Second, the desired rate of turnover for the department where shampoo is stocked and sold will have been determined. Third, allowances will have been made for the length of time between ordering periods, for the time needed to get the order to the supplier or warehouse, shipping time, time in transit, and a safety factor for unanticipated delays. And fourth, minimum packings of the item will have been worked out that are a compromise between the higher costs of small packings and the need for a packing that will permit replenishment in keeping with the display space's capacity.

The individual display space should hold the complete stock of the item. The replenishment schedule will have as one of its prime goals that of avoiding storage of reserve stock under the display space or in an adjoining stockroom. The extra handling, the rental of this additional space, and the chore of keeping track of surplus stock are all expensive. Exceptions to keeping all stock of an item in its special display space will be very bulky items and best-sellers, like facial tissues. Also, items scheduled to be advertised or promoted at special prices will have to be ordered separately in larger quantities and assigned extra reserve stock space. Such exceptions will not lend themselves to the eyeball check, but a great many categories of small, basic, staple items can be replenished by this method and advantage taken of its time-saving short-cuts.

SEEDING

A more mechanized system of replenishment of basic merchandise is the seeding method. Before the manufacturer delivers his merchandise to the retailer, he places a reordering ticket, which is called a seed, in each individual unit package. For example, a manufacturer may insert a reordering ticket in a box containing three skirt plackets of one size and one color. A seed by definition is a unit of reproduction, and that is its function here. It remains in the box at the store until the salesclerk opens it up to replenish a display or rack. At this point, the seed is removed from the box with the merchandise and combined with other seeds to start the replenishment cycle. It is mailed to a central point designated by the manufacturer, where he processes it so that a reorder is created and a new box of three skirt plackets, complete with another seed, is started on its way to the store. The number of individual pieces of merchandise represented by one seed will vary according to the packing unit, which, in turn, depends for its size on the rate of sale of the item and its planned turnover.

There are obvious advantages to seeding over count and recount and eyeball checking. The elimination of counting and checking procedures further reduces clerical costs. Decision-making, even on this elementary level, is limited to the original determination of the size of the ordering unit and its place in the model stock. And the replenishment procedure is started when the unit is first placed on sale, not after it has been depleted. This is important because of irregularities in the rate of sale of even the most staple merchandise. A group of campers might appear one morning and clean out a store's entire stock of flashlight batteries. If replenishment is by the seeding method, a reorder will be generated immediately by the accumulation and return of the seeds to the processing point. On the other hand, replenishment under count and recount and eyeball checking would normally wait for the arbitrary time period set for the ordering cycle to begin.

As a method of reordering merchandise, seeding has not had the success and growth it appears to deserve for a number of reasons. First, the big retailers have not been able to agree on a uniform system. This forces the supplier either to maintain separate inventories for each retailer using a different system, or to assume the costs of placing each retailer's particular seed in each container at the time each order is filled, which causes extra, expensive handling. And many large retailers are not interested in seeding at all, perhaps because they feel that their highly developed warehousing systems of replenishment are adequate, or that the basic, staple type of merchandise most usually seeded is too small a part of their business to warrant training their employees to use this method.

The second reason why seeding has not been more widely adopted for the replenishment of basic merchandise is the persistently high rate of human error in handling the individual seeds. Employee training has failed to cut down the percentage of lost seeds to a desirable level, and the economies of seeding are therefore reduced by the necessity of returning to the count and recount method to bring the stocks back to the model level. If these periodic counts are too infrequent or poorly scheduled, the mishandling of a number of seeds will cause badly unbalanced stocks and lost sales. This vulnerability to out-of-stock conditions when seeds are mishandled is one of the serious drawbacks to the system.

A possible third reason for the limited acceptance of seeding is the concern of manufacturers as to the legality of offering this costly service if some retailers are not interested in it. There is the likelihood that these non-seeding retailers may insist on a comparably valuable service of another kind.

But seeding is working effectively in some areas and its advantages have spurred continuing efforts to realize its benefits more fully. The Association of General Merchandise Chains Inc. has had a committee working on pre-ticketing of merchandise by vendors before shipment to the retailer. This committee is striving to work out a standard reorder ticket that can be either dropped in the item's container or attached by string or pin to a wide variety of products.

Adoption of a uniform ticketing system could lead to the highly desirable goal of pre-ticketing by the vendor at the source. This would lead to the elimination of the present heavy costs of ticketing by the retailer at his warehouse or individual stores. It is also reasonable to expect that if store employees were dealing with a uniform system that applied to a much higher percentage of merchandise handled, they could be so trained that the present high proportion of lost seeding tickets would be greatly reduced.

SALESBOOK STOCK CONTROL

The clerk's salesbook common to most department stores provides a record of the sale of each item. Observing a clerk recording the sale of a $2.00 necktie in triplicate must impress anyone with the high cost of such a method of accumulating sales data. Moreover, each of the carbon copies of the sales slips will have to be reviewed later to complete the classification of sales and the stock replenishment procedure. While it is true that the average sale by the department store clerk will far exceed $2.00 and the percentage cost of triplicate salesbook recording will decrease accordingly, the advantage of replacing such cumbersome procedures with automatic systems is obvious. In any low-cost, mass-merchandise operation, mechanization is absolutely necessary.

VENDOR IN-STORE STOCK CONTROL

There are important classifications of merchandise in which the manufacturer has found it to his advantage to perform the stock control function at the individual store with his own staff, even though this is a very expensive undertaking for him. Vendor in-store stock control is being employed in such categories as greeting cards, children's books, and cosmetic lines. In food stores, categories such as baby foods are often serviced in this way.

Manufacturers most often seek to control those lines whose sales volume is big enough to carry the extra cost of paying field representatives to travel and call on individual stores. The line is usually broad and extensive, and would be likely to present housekeeping problems at stores without this specialized attention on the part of the manufacturer. The chosen line must be broadly distributed in enough stores so that field representatives do not have to travel long distances between calls. Field representatives will be most productive in categories where there is frequent change of item, requiring frequent adjustment of listing and display space. Greeting cards and children's drawing and crayon books are good examples of such lines. Stores may have trouble keeping up with the many changes in these items without manufacturer assistance.

A dominant brand in a very competitive field may be forced to offer this store-level assistance to its outlets to maintain its control in the bitter fight for more space and better display. Another reason why manufacturers are willing to pay handsomely to control certain lines is that they may have a special problem in salesclerk as well as in consumer education. For example, the introduction of a new line of cosmetic items will benefit if the product's selling points are explained directly to the store's personnel. Regular checkups will guarantee a high minimum quality of display and a completeness of stocks that most stores cannot be depended upon to achieve. Manufacturer's field representatives will have the opportunity to remove shopworn and slow-selling items that are clogging the distribution channels by occupying space unproductively, and perhaps deterring the store from ordering and selling the fastest-selling items in the line. Also, a manufacturer with a field force is in a preferred position to test the marketing and display of new products and to follow up their introduction.

The Buyer's Role

To a large extent, the buyer's function in establishing merchandise assortments and model stocks in categories where such in-store control is available has been taken over by the manufacturer. The wise buyer for stores with a limited amount of skilled personnel, who is aware of the number of sales that are being lost in various categories because special attention is not being given, will be most interested in this field service. Of course, he will have less control over a category when the manufacturer is directly managing the assortment and its display.

Since this type of in-store stock control usually involves a rack or display space of fixed size, the buyer must be sure that the brand or line is strong enough to deserve exclusive use of this space. He must regularly weigh the sales and profit production of the line in relation to alternative use of that space.

The buyer must also resist over-stocking to keep investment in line with sales and planned turnover. A short-sighted field representative, possibly paid by commission on sales or working to earn a sales quota award, may load a store's inventory needlessly. The buyer must be sure that the field service is adequate to maintain stocks and sales. Even the normal amount of fallibility in a vendor's field organization will cause some missed schedules, out-of-stock conditions, and misunderstandings and disagreements with store personnel.

Ideally, most buying-merchandising teams will prefer to control the inventory and display of their lines themselves. Practically,

91

however, they will know that the store organizations of most mass merchandisers are so limited by time and by wage expenses that they cannot cope with some lines of merchandise adequately to get satisfactory results. The buyer must know his stores' capabilities so well that he will be able to determine when he should use in-store vendor services and when he should work through the store organization only.

6

The Buyer and the Computer

The unhappy truth is that most buyers have so much routine and clerical work to do that they must neglect their more important, creative functions. Recent surveys show that even in well-run departments a buyer spends from one-quarter to one-third of his average day on routine tasks. And it is not uncommon to find situations where 80 percent or even 90 percent of the buyer's work load is routine. . . . The great promise of purchasing by computer is that it will take over the buyer's routine work, perform it faster and more accurately than he can, and leave him free for complex decision-making and other creative activities.[1]

A recent trade magazine advertisement pictured a very overweight male customer with a bathroom scale in his arms. The caption asks, "He's about to buy the last Model A26 bathroom scale in your stock and you won't know it until another customer asks for one. What are you going to do about it?"[2] The response of the retailer still restricted in his replenishment system to a once-a-month ordering schedule is obvious. He is not likely to do anything about the sale of his last bathroom scale until it is time to reorder that category.

The advantages of control systems that quickly feed back to the

[1]J. William Widing, Jr. and C. Gerald Diamond, "Buy by Computer," *Harvard Business Review,* March-April 1964, p. 111.

[2]Sweda International in *The Discount Merchandiser,* March 1969, back cover.

buyer sales information of this type are tremendous. Imagine the joy of the retailer who has achieved a completely automated stock control system! Never again will he be out-of-stock on wanted merchandise. Never again will his money be tied up in excessive quantities of slower-selling inventory. IBM has estimated that for every $100 spent in a store, another $90 would have been spent had the customer's needs been fully met. The computer promises to provide inventory controls that will enable the customer to find just what she wants without over-stocking of any item by the store. Visions of this beautiful dream-world explain the great interest and investment in computers by all mass merchandisers in recent years.

Suppose a retailer has had annual sales of bathroom scales totaling $6,000 with an average investment of $2,000. His turnover of stock and investment, then, was three times during that year. Assume further that a computerized control plan has achieved the same annual sales with half as much stock on hand, or $1,000. Stock-turn has therefore increased from three times to six times and the retailer is free to use the uninvested $1,000 as additional capital in other areas. It is also probable that his sales of bathroom scales will have increased substantially because of the maintenance of complete stocks. Perhaps he will have achieved sales of $7,500 with an investment of only $1,000. Peak seasonal demands may have been discovered that were unsuspected under a once-a-month reordering schedule.

Obviously, a machine that yields a full, accurate record of the movement of merchandise into the hands of consumers demands the understanding of the buyer. And the buyer must be acutely aware of the computer's present and potential impact on his functions.

THE COMPUTER

A computer is a machine that records, stores, and classifies information at miraculous speeds. The buyer need not possess a detailed understanding of what is put into the computer or of exactly how it is processed. But he must know enough about the machine and about electronic data processing (commonly referred to as EDP) to understand the reports issued by the computer and to be able to communicate with the computer specialist in determining which reports will be most useful.

The computer has been well described as another in a long line of devices created to figure out problems of counting and mathematics. Mankind has used the multiplication tables effectively for centuries. The abacus has been employed as a counting mechanism far back in history. The adding machine was an important step forward in the management of figures. The electric adding machine performed even more complicated tasks at greater speed, and was followed by the development of electronic tabulating equipment which "stored" information on punched cards capable of being sorted and classified mechanically. The computer is the latest in this series of historical developments.

The ultimate capacities of the computer for solving retail problems are still unknown, but it has already been demonstrated that it can turn out answers to questions that were not even practical to ask several years ago. And the computer is capable of building stock control systems and providing information feedback that can revolutionize the buying function. It is the most efficient method yet invented for the gathering up of records of sales transactions or merchandise movement to be examined by those responsible for projecting future sales and for determining the stocks best designed to capture those sales.

Computer Input

Input is the information fed into the computer. For example, suppose it has been agreed to keep track of the stocks and movement of bathroom scales by recording receipts of shipments into the warehouse or store, adding these receipts to any existing stocks to determine total stocks, and recording withdrawals from warehouse stocks or from store stocks by sale. The computer can receive this input information in several ways:

Punched Cards. Holes are punched into cards by a key-punch machine operator in an arrangement that is keyed to be "read" by the computer. This card with information stored in its particular combination of punched holes is then placed in a stack with other cards for later classification and use.

Magnetic Tape. The holes in punched cards may be converted into signals on a magnetic tape, which can be picked up much more quickly by the computer than information from punched cards; or punched cards may be bypassed completely by putting information directly on magnetic tape.

Punched Paper Tape. This is a refinement of the familiar cash register tape so widely used to record individual retail sales. The wanted information is punched into the tape at the time of the sale in a form that a computer can read. Machines that record this punched paper tape can be attached to various types of business equipment, such as adding and accounting machines.

Optical Scanning. In this procedure, computers actually "read" hand-written or printed material. Hand-written material must be in stylized characters, which are, however, simple and easily taught to clerks. After the input information is either written in these stylized characters or printed in cash register or adding machine tapes, it is delivered to the computer which reads it "optically." This scanning method eliminates the need to transfer the original input information onto punched cards and makes possible the direct classification of sales records by the computer. In stores where sales are recorded by checkout cash registers, the checker indexes the sold item's classification as she records the dollar amount of the sale. In stores or departments where items like furniture and refrigerators are recorded individually on sales slips, the salesclerk will have been instructed in the writing of the essential input information in the stylized characters necessary for computer reading.

Chains with stores spread over a large geographical area have the problem of feeding the original input information developed by any of the above systems into computers that may be located at a central point thousands of miles away from the individual outlets.

The high cost of computers, whether leased, shared with other companies, or owned, precludes having such equipment at more than one or two points. Since speed is usually essential to the effectiveness of any computer feedback system, telephone or teletype may be used for transmission. In unusual instances where speed is not an important factor, information may be mailed. In local areas close to the computer, messenger service would be employed. Since electronic transmission costs are high, retailers usually send the day's sales or ordering information to the centrally-located computer late at night, when transmission costs are cheapest.

Improvements and refinements of input systems are being developed at a rapid rate. The costs of these systems are high but so are the rewards, and the incentive to develop them grows each time the wage cost of running manual systems increases, or competent manpower becomes more scarce.

The Programming and Processing of Data

Before the computer can process the delivered input data it must be told what information management wants and in what form. This setting up of the computer to perform a particular function is called "programming." The programmer is a specialist who must know the exact capabilities of the computer to produce wanted information; be able to relate the time and cost of delivering the information to its value; have the ability to communicate with management in working out the most meaningful reports in the clearest form; and be able to translate this program into computer language.

Suppose management is using a computerized warehouse stock control system that records the beginning inventory, adds receipts of new shipments, gives total stock on hand, and deducts reported sales of the item. With this basic information, the buying-merchandising team will reorder according to a predetermined basic stock and turnover plan. Though all of this information is available from less-mechanized stock control systems, the computer will supply it more quickly and accurately. And it is likely that the buyer will be receiving information that he never would have sought without the computer—information that would have been available only from costly physical counts or by sifting mountains of records. For example, a computer's comparison of sales in one quarter of the year with the other three quarters, over a several-year period, might reveal a seasonal peak that could be exploited by promotion. Without the computer such information would have been extremely difficult and costly to obtain. As buyers develop proficiency with these new tools, additional profitable uses will come to light.

Computer Output

Of the many types of reports that a computer can spew out, the following will be the most interesting and valuable to the buying-merchandising team:

Product Movement. This report may have been programmed to measure directly the retail sales of the previous day, week, or month. Or it may be a record of movement from the warehouse to the point of sale for a specified period. In either case, the computer will certainly be supplying this information faster than any other system.

Profit Comparisons. Reports programmed to show cost and retail prices, as well as item movement, will also print out the gross dollar profit. The availability of this additional figure makes possible a comparison of profit by item and category. This figure may reveal that a low-priced, short-profit item with higher volume is producing considerably less gross profit dollars than the slower-selling, high-priced, high-markon item. It will make it possible to measure the impact of a price-cut promotion by determining, for example, whether the increased sales volume will more than make up for the sacrifice of profit per unit sold.

Effectiveness of Display Methods. The merchandiser may solve a problem involving the display or location of a category by measuring results in two groups of stores that have been assigned to test alternate methods. For example, the effectiveness of a mass display in piled-up full cartons may be weighed against the impact of a more attractive display.

Sales Promotion Results. Advertising programs will always have the institutional value of bringing the store's name and image to the attention of the potential customer. But a detailed measurement of the productivity of each ad in relation to its cost is likely to be a very inexact procedure. Fast, detailed computer reports of item movement as well as comparisons with previous reports will be very helpful in the planning of promotions and advertising.

Vendor Analysis. Which manufacturer of a particular category is doing the best job? Does a comparison with previous months or years demonstrate that one vendor's line is showing significantly greater growth than his competitors' and should, therefore, be merchandised more aggressively? Is it true that the national advertising of one brand more than justifies its higher cost to the retailer and the resulting short markup? Or does the record show that better promotion of an unadvertised brand of lower cost will produce more profit? Does a computer report of sales and profit by an individual vendor indicate the desirability of greater concentration of purchases on a particular manufacturer? Does a report of comparative delivery times point to a supplier with an unusually erratic record that is causing out-of-stocks?

Out-of-Line Stocks. A computer may report items over-stocked in relation to current demand or items dangerously low in quantity. The excesses may be sufficient to justify reshipment to the vendor or to other store locations. Or they may indicate correctable errors in judgment or in the forecasting of sales. Inventories that are too low may reflect an unforeseeable special demand, failure to forecast properly, or simply a clerical or mechanical error that calls for a special order.

Order Writing. Computers are often programmed to go beyond the production of stock control figures to the actual writing of the replenishment orders for the merchandise. In the case of the most basic items with steady, predictable demand, order-writing may be 100 percent mechanical. Reorder points will have been established in advance based on rate of sale and planned turnover, and such minor factors as packing quantity and minimum shipment requirements will be in the program. But there are so many possible variables affecting the movement of an item that some buyer review is usually desirable. Truckload requirements, extra discounts for special periods, alternate packs, temporary substitutions, promotional tie-ins, current market information not yet recorded by the computer, or sales trends up or down that might adjust the buying arithmetic will usually require the special attention of the buyer. However, such variables may also be programmed for the computer if they are frequent or constant enough to warrant it.

Management Control of Buying. Fast, accurate reporting of stock conditions will also give the merchandise manager and top management the facts for better control of the buyer's activities. Buying errors will be more visible to management, and, therefore, more easily corrected. And management may recognize merchandising opportunities that the buyer may have overlooked.

THE COMPUTER IN ACTION

Not only are the computers themselves extremely costly to purchase or rent, but their programming, supplies and forms are also very expensive. To be practical, such large expenditures must bear a relationship to the dollar value of the item being recorded.

For example, it is reasonable to expect that a mass merchandiser using computers will record each individual sale of TV sets. A sale of several hundred dollars can clearly "afford" to carry the costs of the computer report and of the mechanics of replacing the sold item on the store's shelves. Similarly, the sale of a moderately-priced lady's handbag will be recorded individually. Since computer recording costs are the same for both the TV set and the handbag, the cost in proportion to the retail value of the handbag will be higher. However, the element of style makes the prompt reporting of the handbag sale even more urgent.

100

But computer stock control of a 79¢ extension cord for the TV set and of a 98¢ change purse to fit the handbag presents different problems. Individual sales records of such low-priced items may well be too expensive to maintain. Here, stock movement and condition will probably be reported back to the buyer in the form of a record of warehouse shipments. Not only is the cost of collecting and reporting the individual sales of small items often prohibitive, but the buyer may not want such detailed information to replenish his stock.

To illustrate the functioning of a comparatively simple and unsophisticated computer system, we will follow the replenishment of a 79¢ extension cord, which is a staple, basic part of the stock of a group of stores serviced by a central warehouse.

Replenishment Order. Store A, operating under its normal system of replenishment of low-priced, basic stocks, has reported that it needs 24 pieces of 79¢ extension cords. The store's reorder clerk had made an eyeball check of the pegboard hook on which this particular extension cord is displayed and found the model stock to be depleted to the planned reorder point.

Computer Input. The store's requirement becomes computer input at the warehouse or other computer location. The information may have reached the computer by hole-punched cards, magnetic tape, punched paper tape, or by optical scanning of written forms or lists.

Invoice. The computer, performing as programmed, creates an invoice for the transaction, probably combining it with orders for other items from the same store. Copies of the invoice will be made simultaneously for the warehouseman, who will pick the order and pack it, and, probably, for the trucker as a bill of lading.

Adjusting Warehouse Inventory. The computer will deduct the 24 pieces ordered from the total warehouse inventory of the item so that a perpetual count of warehouse stocks is always maintained. It will also be prepared to report the total withdrawals of the item for any predetermined period of time.

101

Warehouse Out-of-Stock. If the extension cord was out-of-stock when ordered, the computer, without any further clerical work, will "remember" that 24 pieces were ordered by Store A but not shipped, and when a new shipment arrives at the warehouse, it will fill this back-order and invoice it.

Out-of-Stock Reports. Meanwhile the computer will probably have been programmed to report the out-of-stock condition to the buyer who may then expedite delivery. The store manager may also receive weekly reports of items he had previously ordered but had not been sent so that he may avoid duplication of orders. As a further safeguard against duplication and overstocks, the computer may be set up to reject a second order for the back-ordered item.

Price-Marking. Input of the order may also have been programmed to trigger the store's price-marking system. The correct quantity of stickers, tags, or labels will have been printed for attachment either at the warehouse or at the store, if needed.

Reports for Buyer. The buyer will have available to him a computer report, probably weekly, of the movement of extension cords from the warehouse to the stores, and of stocks remaining on hand at the warehouse. Also available to him will be comparisons by month, quarter, or year of past movement as a basis for merchandising judgments.

THE ADVANTAGES OF THE COMPUTER TO THE BUYER

It has already been noted that the proper programming of the computer will facilitate merchandise control and deliver a continuing flow of sales information to the buyer that will enable him to maintain inventories at the desired level with greater accuracy. The rush of retailers to secure these operating and cost-cutting advantages is understandable. There are also other ways in which the computer benefits the buyer.

The speed and capacity of the computer make it economically

feasible for the buyer to break down or classify his merchandise lines in manageable segments that conform to customer usage and interest. Buyers in computer-less companies, on the other hand, will probably be forced to work with very broad classifications of merchandise because further breakdowns would be available only through arduous personal record-keeping and counting. The buyer of bathroom scales who knows only the dollar sales and inventory amount for the entire appliance grouping is obviously at a great disadvantage compared with the fortunate buyer whose computer is programmed to give him the same figures by item or small groups of items, and in units as well as in dollars.

The availability of precise information by classification is also of great value in executive decision-making. When all furniture is classified together in an inadequate system, restrictions might be placed on the further purchase of, say, bedroom furniture, because the store had an excess of lawn furniture. This is precisely how investments were controlled in many large companies b.c.—before computers.

The buying-merchandising team will be more concerned with what the computer can report on the status of inventory than with all other reports combined. The computer replaces guesswork and grinding, time-consuming arithmetic with fast and accurate scientific fact-finding. The future leaders in the mass-merchandising field will be those who pioneer in the systematic control of their stocks. Since every retailer will be eagerly seeking the advantages of computerization, it will be absolutely necessary to achieve such control just to keep up with the competition.

The quicker availability of more accurate information will also enable the buyer to pinpoint his problem areas, both in sales and in stock control. He will be more readily able to identify trends within his merchandise classifications. Increases or decreases in the popularity of an item will stand out more clearly and call for action. Quick detection of growing popularity will help the buyer make the most of the opportunity. Quick detection of declining popularity will help him reduce the quantity of slow-selling stocks and mark-downs. To assist the buyer with his purchasing, the computer will supply him with adequate information to select markets in which a particular category has greater popularity. Accurate, quick computer information also permits a greater centralization of buying. Before computerization, much of the purchasing was done by area buying supervisors simply because the necessary feedback of information to the central buying office was too slow and too meagre for the home office buyer to do a good job.

When combined, all of the advantages of the computer to the buying operation will reduce by several days the total time between the sale of an item in a store and the arrival of its replacement at the point of sale. This reduction of merchandise "turnaround" time is especially important in the fashion area.

It is clear that the stakes are high. Frank Burnside, president of a department store in Wilkes-Barre, Pennsylvania, estimated that "centrally produced weekly classification merchandise position reports . . . will cost about one-fifth of one percent of sales. If the buyer's management makes such data available to him, the expected reduction in average cost inventory investment will be 20 percent." He further predicted that this and other resulting benefits of improved control would add up to an increase in net profit of 20 to 25 percent.[3]

Freeing the Buyer's Time

The degree to which the buyer's time will be freed by the computer will vary among categories and departments. The buyer of apparel, with its highly volatile demand, will not be helped in the area of mechanical placement of reorders to the same extent as the buyer of small hardware, but he will benefit even more from the feedback of sales information.

E. B. Weiss, an articulate, outspoken critic and analyst of advertising and retailing, predicts flatly that the computer will turn the buyer into an automaton: "There are few functions in business more susceptible to electronic statistical control than the buying function. And EDP (electronic data processing) is making such rapid advances among mass retailers that there is just not the slightest room to doubt that, within three to five years, it will be

[3] "Merchandising by Classification," *The Buyer's Manual, op. cit.,* p. 191.

dominating the buyer to at least the same degree as does the buying committee . . . it will be the electronic machine that will be making a substantial part of the decisions. The buyer will merely convey that decision to the supplier."[4]

Mr. Weiss' 1962 predictions have not come true. Not only has the rush to computerize buying been slower than he had anticipated, but indications are that the quality of the change in buying has been and will be different from what Mr. Weiss expected. Freed from much of the routine and mechanical aspects of his job, the buyer will have the time to be more of an executive. Liberated from paper-shuffling tasks, he can focus on better buying, product development, value-building, getting out into the market, and, perhaps, on creating private brand programs as well. And the computer will be supplying fresh information from which the buyer can develop more sophisticated and more profitable stock controls.

As the computer moves deeper and deeper into buying and takes over more and more of the routine functions, it is probable that the buyer will cover a greater number of merchandise categories. This may mean some consolidation of buying jobs, and, therefore, fewer buyers. But the buying job itself will be upgraded and require skills and a performance level beyond those of pre-computer days.

The best buyers and merchandisers are scarce and expensive, like all best-qualified personnel. The more buying decisions can be reduced to formula and mechanics, the lower the buying costs. One of management's strong incentives in the development of electronic data processing is to implement this economy.

Factors Limiting the Effectiveness of the Computer

The impact of the computer on our age has been compared with that of the Industrial Revolution on its times. Seers prophesy computers with I.Q. scores of 150. Observers point out that retailing is

---

[4] E. B. Weiss, *The Vanishing Salesman* (New York: McGraw-Hill Book Company, 1961), p. 93 Copyright © McGraw-Hill Book Company. Used with permission.

finally taking belated recognition of the profit-making values of computer research that manufacturing has been cashing in on for years. Surely no advance could be more happily greeted than the optimistic promise to establish order in the retail jungle. What, then, is delaying the progress to this retailing paradise? Why hasn't scientific fact-finding more completely replaced the haphazard guesswork and ivory-tower decision-making so characteristic of much of retailing?

The obstacles are as much man-made as machine-made. Human reluctance and inability to adapt have limited the success of the computer as much as the limitations of the machine itself. In the area of stock control, there is little opposition to computerization by buyer-merchandisers, but in the buying area, they instinctively tend to resist the intrusion of computers and to over-emphasize the intuitive, non-routine facets of buying. Programmers of computer systems are familiar with an attitude among buying and merchandising personnel that borders on hostility and downright uncooperativeness. Buyers may have convinced management that their functions are mostly non-routine and that large expenditures for computers in the purchasing area would not be productive. The computer may arouse fear and confusion in those unfamiliar with it. Will it eliminate their jobs, eventually if not right now? Will it make their jobs more difficult and expose areas of inadequacy? Will it make a dull, routine job out of a satisfying one? Management officials who have risen from the bottom of the merchandising ranks may be somewhat sympathetic to this attitude. They may not fully comprehend the new system and its value and may, therefore, unconsciously resist it. They may also have been disillusioned by the failure of such older systems as punched cards to achieve adequate stock control. Moreover, the financial administrators, rather than the merchandisers, may be in charge of the introduction of the computer program, and they would be more likely to develop the areas which they know best before phasing in the buying operation with which they are less familiar. There are many human factors of this sort which impede the fuller and faster development of the computer in stock control.

Some progressive companies have recognized and met the need

for better cooperation between the merchandising and computer teams by appointing a merchandising information officer with a solid understanding of the problems of both groups. It is his role to improve communication and understanding through education, training, explanation, and perhaps even discipline. He can be very valuable in seeing to it that lack of communication does not prevent the programmer from setting up a system of maximum value to the merchandising team. A competent liaison man of this sort can greatly speed the progress and maximize the effectiveness of a computer program.

The continuing rate of progress in computer development is astonishing and any assessment of the computer's future possibilities would be pure crystal-ball gazing. But certain basic, inherent man-versus-machine conflicts must be recognized and examined.

Though the computer cannot completely replace the buyer even in the control and purchase of such routine items as paper clips, it will free him from much of the manual arithmetic of stock control and supply him with data that he probably didn't have before computerization, with the result that he will be able to control paper clips more speedily and efficiently than ever before. But he will still have to negotiate alternate items and sources.

At the other end of the buying spectrum, the apparel buyer of the most non-routine categories must have intimate, personal contact with his suppliers on a daily basis, as well as an up-to-the-minute knowledge of his market and ever-shifting demand. The value of the computer to the apparel buyer, in addition to the facts it supplies, is the time that it gives him to work personally with manufacturers in the development of products and sources. It is safe to say that any future computer development cannot conceivably replace him although they will surely help him in unpredictable ways.

A computer is not a brain. Its output can only be as good as the human thought that went into its programming, and its product can only be as valuable to the buyer-merchandiser as the use to which he puts it. If the information is not analyzed and applied, it is not worth the reams of paper on which it is printed. Its high cost makes it imperative that its value be exploited to the maximum, through the cooperative efforts of the engineers and merchandisers. The buyer who is suddenly deluged with daily information that he had formerly received weekly or monthly, or not at all, may be at a loss as to how to use it most effectively. Management specialists may be needed to guide him in this area. Research in depth in areas of stock control and buying may be very foreign to a buying-merchandising team's thinking and considerable orientation may be required before the maximum value can be gained from such new, sophisticated information systems.

A much wider communications gap than that between the buyer and computer teams is the one that exists between store and computer management. Because of the almost total lack of contact between these two groups, store management has a very hazy idea of the system itself or its goals. But the computer's mistakes are long remembered; and there are usually a few big, well-publicized ones in the early stages of any computerization program. Suspicion and criticism have their roots in lack of understanding and communication. This situation has been aptly illustrated by trade magazine cartoonists. In one cartoon, a manager and his assistant survey rows of empty display counters. The caption is, "The way I get it, the machine burped and just forgot to send us this month's order." In another cartoon, the store manager waves his arms in despair among counters piled six feet high with dolls and says to a programmer, "Whadaya mean the machine can't make a mistake!"[5] Obviously, computer systems will progress more rapidly when such communications gaps are bridged.

Another deterrent to computer progress in mass retailing is management's past record of misunderstanding and misapplying statistics in general. Statistics are too frequently used out of context to attack or defend a position, rather than analyzed without bias for the light they can shed. For example, markon figures are readily available to the smallest merchant without much mechanical assistance. But markon can be too high and drive customers away, or too low and result in sales without profit; it may also fail to take

[5]"Learning to Live with the Computer," *Chain Store Age*, March 1969, pp. 40-41.

into account special competitive or other local operating conditions. Without such qualifying facts, the markon percentage statistic can be very misleading. It tends to be overemphasized, however, because it is readily available while the qualifying facts are not. Another statistic that is easily arrived at and often abused because of its availability is wage cost as a percentage of sales. What may be regarded in a distant central office as progress in reducing the wage cost may actually cripple the store's operation, encourage pilfering, and result in smaller net profits. Thus, improperly qualified statistics may conceal facts as well as reveal them. The common misuse of statistics by retailers will continue to be a factor in the postponement of the realization of all the values to be gained from the computer, but these values will increase as merchants become better educated in the use of quicker and more accurate information.

The computer can forecast and estimate, but not predict or foretell. It can assemble and present facts to the merchandising team that will enable this group to apply its know-how more effectively, but it cannot think. Clearly, what is needed is a proper mixture of computers and people. It is just as wrong for management officials to be so much in awe of their computers that they neglect human judgment as it was for them to operate in pre-computer days without accurate records—by the seats of their pants. Rigid computer-devised plans for stock control and open-to-buy quotas may be too restrictive: "At best open-to-buy is based on a series of guesses, and moderate violations should not only be permitted but sometimes encouraged. For only then will the imaginative, inspired merchant be able to swing for the fences while his more timid counterpart is merely bunting. . . . The very existence of open-to-buy calls for *sound* risk-taking on the part of those who choose to stretch its dictates."[6]

Some Opinions on the Computer

As experience piles up and system refinements develop, many

[6]Abe Jacobsen, "On Open-to-Buy," *The Discount Merchandiser,* June 1969, p. 40.

wise words on the values and limitations of the computer for retailers are being written by thoughtful retailing authorities.

Dr. M. S. Mayer observes: "EDP can see no further than the point of purchase, and it is blind to those facts which are not machinable. . . . EDP scans the store rather than the intention to purchase, the transaction rather than the person and the customer rather than the consumer. . . . It tells the merchant about sales rather than the shoppers, and about merchandise rather than markets. . . . In short, EDP lacks what we would call vision—a peculiarly human activity, which is as necessary to the progress of a company as the electricity that powers the computers." [7]

Ben Gordon writes: "When we surrender decision-making . . . to the magic of printouts, the computer can be an instrument of corporate freeze. . . . The computer is brilliantly informative but it cannot conceive. It cannot innovate. When it assumes command it tends to perpetuate its own experience. . . . The real function of the computer . . . is to liberate management from the drudgery of decision-making on the maintenance level, so that more time can be devoted to the doodle-pad of pure innovative movement. Otherwise we become tenders instead of builders." [8]

Grey Matter Comments: "Scientific approach will be the essential background of the retail management executive. . . . BUT new research techniques will *not* provide one vital ingredient of retailing success: the human element. Call it 'brains,' 'judgment,' 'ability,' or what you will. . . . Insight and imagination will remain one of the most precious assets of retail management. . . . Improved research techniques will create a better climate for decision-making, but it will still take inspired imaginative *thinking* to use the new tools effectively." [9]

[7] As quoted by Nathaniel Schwartz, editor-in-chief of *The Discount Merchandiser,* March 1969.

[8] "Computer or Doodle Pad," *Chain Store Age,* August 1968, p. 31.

[9] *Grey Matter, Retail Edition,* May 1963.

Marvin Bower points out: "The revolution in planning and management information is still in its early stages. But it is already becoming trite to observe that the computer is turning the revolution into an explosion. . . . However, every system of management must meet the ultimate test of how effectively it causes people to decide and act." [10]

To the buying-merchandising team, the computer brings a magnificent new tool for stock control and a bonanza of quick, accurate information which can transform buying techniques. With a full understanding of the many factors impeding and limiting the computer's development, its great potential makes it imperative that the buyer welcome the concept of computerization 100 percent—that he not fight it. The buyer must ignore disaster reports of computer errors, accepting them as part of the price that must be paid for a new, unfolding development in a transitional period. He must hasten the progress and benefits of the computer by exploiting its potential rather than waiting passively for performance results, and he must sell the concept of computerization to others by his example. Finally, the buyer must help to build cooperation between the computer technicians and the buying-merchandising team itself. Technicians sometimes forget that they are tools, not principals, of management; and buyers often see themselves as too diverse, varied, and spread out in their functions for computerization. Progress requires cooperative interaction.

It has been reported that this sign hangs on the wall of the IBM office in Tokyo:

MAN—SLOW, SLOVENLY, BRILLIANT
IBM—FAST, ACCURATE, STUPID

[10]Marvin Bower, *The Will to Manage* (New York: McGraw-Hill Book Company, 1966), p. 222. Copyright © McGraw-Hill Book Company. Used with permission.

7

The Buyer's Responsibility for
Merchandise and Expense Control

. . . In our work of merchandising statistics, merchandising strategy, complicated promotional techniques and high demands on maintained markup, [buyer] talents must be teamed up with those of the controller.

We need sensible chance takers, inventory analysts, customer satisfiers, customer magnets.

These men don't travel alone. They should be riding tandem with the controller.[1]

Many important elements of retail profit with which the buyer must be concerned require close cooperation with the controller and financial division. Directives and guidelines emanate from this division on such vital subjects as pricing, markdowns, investment, turnover, discounts, and expense control.

The buyer and the controller tend to approach the ultimate goal of net profit from opposite positions. The buying-merchandising team thinks in terms of "more"—more sales, more promotion, more advertising, more buying; the controller and his staff are more likely to think in terms of "less"—less expense, less investment, less markdowns, less wage cost. If either the merchandiser or the

---

[1] Abe Jacobsen, "On Controllers and Merchandisers," *The Discount Merchandiser,* August 1968, p. 32.

112

controller is allowed to dominate, the entire operation will be seriously unbalanced and handicapped. The name of the game is selling; but sales can be profitless when selling costs are uncontrolled. On the other hand, a dollar cut from expense contributes a dollar to net profit; but expense cutting that reduces the opportunity to sell merchandise may reduce profit as well. A balance of authority and a smooth working relationship between the merchandising and financial divisions are vital to the success of chain retail companies.

All merchandising personnel, whether they be store employees, buyers, divisional merchandise managers, or merchandising vice presidents, instinctively strive for increased sales above all else because of their training, and usually because of their sales-oriented compensation. All of them are sometimes tempted to rationalize low markon, over-investment, expensive promotion, and the uneconomic use of display space as productive of sales without properly considering the true costs of securing these sales.

On the other hand, in their zeal to save money, cut costs, and show improved figures, the controller and his staff are sometimes prone to eliminate expense in one area that pops up less obtrusively in another. Specialized operations, wisely conceived to perform a minor function with greater efficiency, are easy targets in an economy drive when the function can be buried in a larger operation where it is then done in obscurity with less efficiency and at greater expense. A meat-axe approach to expense budgets may make temporary heroes out of the controller's division, but improper evaluations sometimes lead to the elimination of operations and personnel whose contributions to net profit and overall efficiency justified the expense. The buyer who thoroughly understands the difference between profitable and unprofitable sales, and who communicates and cooperates with his controller's division, will achieve a higher level of net profit for his company.

THE NET PROFIT STATEMENT

Here is an example of a net profit statement comparing this

year's results with those of last year in a selected department of a mass-merchandising chain of stores.[2]

		This Year	Last Year
A.	Sales	$900,000	$850,000
B.	Gross Margin	$353,000	$355,250
C.	Percent of Gross Margin to Sales	39.2%	41.8%
D.	Markdowns	$ 15,000	$ 14,000
E.	Shrinkage	$ 10,000	$ 10,000
F.	Maintained Gross Margin (B minus D and E)	$328,000	$331,250
G.	Buying Expenses	$ 26,000	$ 25,000
H.	Advertising	$ 5,000	$ 5,000
I.	All Other Expenses and Overhead	$270,000	$260,000
J.	Total Expenses (G plus H plus I)	$301,000	$290,000
K.	Net Profit (F minus J)	$ 27,000	$ 41,250
L.	Percent of Net Profit to Sales	3.0%	4.9%

The least experienced buyer or student will see at once from this condensed statement that a small increase in sales this year has not only produced less gross margin, but that much higher expenses and overhead have cut the department's net profit drastically. Detailed information is usually supplied frequently enough so that the buying-merchandising team responsible for this unsatisfactory statement would have been amply forewarned. A retailer who is surprised by such bad news at the year's end either has an inadequate statistical reporting system or simply hasn't been paying attention. The buying-merchandising team that seeks out and studies all the information that the controller's division supplies will find clues that will substantially improve results. Effective action depends much more on the accurate interpretation of figures than on occasionally accurate hunches.

Gross Margin and Pricing for a Profit

Retail profit is derived from the difference between what an article is bought for by the retailer and what he sells it for to the

[2] For the retailing beginner, and for those wishing to pin down their definitions more closely, a Glossary of Retailing Terminology is provided at the end of this book.

customer. If an item costs $2.00 and sells for $3.00, the gross margin is $1.00. This $1.00 must cover all the expenses incurred in selling the article, and still yield a net profit sufficient to justify the owner's investment of capital. For comparison purposes and ease of averaging, gross margin is usually described in terms of retail selling price. In this case, it is the percentage of $1.00 to $3.00, or 33-1/3 percent. This percentage is generally referred to as "markon." Markon percentages will vary widely among merchandise categories, from about 10 percent for staple, quick-turnover items like milk and bread, to well over 50 percent for high-fashion ladies' dresses. This 10 to 50 percent markon spread has been determined from retailing experience to be necessary to cover the varying costs incurred between the time of purchase by the retailer from the supplier and the ultimate purchase by the consumer.

The net profit statement above shows the buyer's department with a 39.2 percent gross margin this year compared with 41.8 percent for the previous year. Suppose that available figures of comparable retailers in the same merchandise category show this year's gross margin to be 40.7 percent. What, then, should be some of the conclusions drawn from these data by the buyer and his superiors?

If all departments of the chain have a similarly bad record this year compared with last year, then the department in our example is just one reflection of an overall merchandising plan that went awry. But if the other departments performed as planned, then perhaps the merchandise in that one department had been bought in the wrong mixture to achieve the planned gross margin and it therefore failed to make its anticipated contribution to the net profit of all the other departments. Or, since our example shows a slight sales improvement but $3,250 less in gross margin dollars, perhaps pricing alone had been over-used as a weapon in selling. If either diagnosis is correct, the buyer should set about to improve the sale of his wares, not by low pricing, but by upgrading the attractiveness and timeliness of his selections.

Price-cutting can be a quick and effective method of attracting customers and moving large quantities of merchandise. But it is a double-edged sword that can also lead to so low a gross margin that selling expenses are not covered and a net loss results. Low prices and big savings have won great popularity for the mass merchant, and this reputation must be nurtured and maintained. Some retailers with very low costs of operations may thrive on the volume generated by underselling their competition on almost everything, but most merchandisers find it necessary to cut prices and promote low-profit items very selectively in order to achieve a mixture that yields a reasonable net profit after all expenses. The buyer's superiors and the controller's division will have supplied budgeted goals. To reach these goals, the buyer should improve sales with judiciously bought special values and with lowered prices in the proper proportion to the sale of regular, more profitable goods.

Indiscriminate slashing of prices to undersell competition on all items at all times may create excitement and additional volume, but it cannot be maintained against any reasonably efficient competition. On the other hand, retailers whose popularity has been built largely on their reputation for low prices and discounting cannot move into much higher gross margin areas without endangering their valuable image.

Of course, discounting does not necessarily have to reduce profit dollars if it results in enough added sales volume, and, indeed, much of the success of the mass merchant comes from this fact. An increase in the sales of an item from $100 to $200 by reducing markon from 35 to 25 percent will produce $50 in gross margin instead of $35 ($100 x 35% = $35 and $200 x 25% = $50). Such overhead costs as rent, heat, and light are not increased by the larger number of transactions, and, therefore, they become a diminished percentage of total volume. There are added costs due to the handling of the additional merchandise sold, but these are minimal in the usual self-service checkout operation. And more customers will probably have been attracted to the store by the discounted merchandise to make other purchases that are more profitable.

Obviously, the pricing of merchandise and the setting of gross margins are vital areas for retailing executives. The successful buyer will learn how to achieve his budgeted figures for gross margin while still employing to the fullest the promotional tools of low price specials and authentic bargins.

Markdowns

A markdown is a reduction of the original retail price of an item. It is a merchandising device used either for promotional purposes or to speed up the disposal of unwanted goods. Markdowns are usually initiated by the central merchandising office when a general, all-store problem arises, but special local clearances will be handled by a store's own management. [3]

The accumulation of unwanted merchandise may be caused by a number of factors, some of which fall within the control of the buyer and could be avoided if he did his job perfectly. These include the following:

Overstocking, or the placement of quantities that are too large for the selling opportunity.

Slow-selling merchandise, or the buying of items that are not as popular as anticipated.

Untimeliness, or the failure to deliver at the proper season or during peak popularity.

Poor pricing, or the attempt to achieve a high gross margin which customers refuse to pay.

Miscellaneous buyer and manufacturer mistakes, including inferior quality, poor patterns, unpopular colors, wrong sizes, poor styling.

Unwanted merchandise ties up investment, restricts funds available to buy wanted merchandise, uses valuable display space, has a negative effect on sales personnel, and lends an image of staleness to assortments. It makes very good sense to quickly dispose of unattractive merchandise and to replace it with fresher,

---

[3]A markdown is thus distinguished from a discount; the latter is a planned reduction of a retail selling price below that intended by the manufacturer, or below the usual price of other retailers, decided on when the merchandise is purchased.

more exciting items. For various reasons, however, this quick, sensible disposal of unwanted goods is often neglected. The buyer, of course, is in no hurry to admit his errors and will be inclined to over-value his purchases and attribute slow movement to the failure of store management to sell skillfully or of staff personnel to promote properly. He may claim that the planned advertising was poorly executed, or that store promotion was less than expected or promised, or that the final decision on pricing was higher than he had recommended.

It is also regrettably true that some retailers are prisoners of their markdown budgets. Markdowns are far from predictable and do not occur in equal, monthly amounts that can be accurately scheduled. Merchandisers, therefore, should not be held to fixed dollar allowances. If a specific markdown makes sense in terms of ultimate greater profit dollars, the markdown budget should be flexible enough to allow for it. Delayed markdown and clearance to fit budget requirements clutter up retailing operations and impede the selling of wanted goods.

Markdowns, then, are a necessary evil in retailing operations. Taken indiscriminately, without a sensible effort to sell out at full markon, they can be a serious and unwarranted drain on profit. On the other hand, a judicious and quick use of lowered prices can be a most effective merchandising tool. The individual buyer should exert as much influence as he has to see to it that markdowns are used in a balanced, intelligent fashion.

Merchandise Dating. There are many good reasons why the price ticket or tag of an item should be imprinted with the date on which the merchandise was received into the stock of a store. It is usually difficult, and often impossible, to determine the exact date of receipt of an item after it has been in the store's stock for some time. Nothing is more helpful in stirring up remedial action on old merchandise than to have its age shown by a simple printed code. The imprinted date may reveal to the store manager or to the visiting supervisor or to the buyer that merchandise is not being properly rotated in the stores—that the clerk is placing the new goods on top of, instead of behind, the old. Uncertainty as to age when a markdown is being considered may frustrate correct action, whereas dating may lead to suggestions of other methods of selling, and, possibly, to the disposal of slow-moving merchandise at full price. Whatever action is taken, dating identifies and focuses attention on the problem. Unfortunately, however, dating costs money, which may turn out to be a significant amount when applied to low-priced and low-profit goods. But where it is practical, dating can be a great aid to effective merchandise control.

OPEN-TO-BUY

Open-to-buy is the dollar value of merchandise that the buyer is authorized to spend within a given period of time. It is a figure agreed upon by his merchandising superiors and the controller's division, and is based on the previous and anticipated performance of his buying division. Open-to-buy may be broken down into separate merchandise categories within a department, or even into specific quantities of individual items, depending on the degree of control that management wishes to exercise. When a computer automatically reorders items to replenish a model stock, the amount needed to bring stocks up to the model quantity is the open-to-buy amount. But we are discussing open-to-buy here in the sense of discretionary purchasing by the buyer, rather than the automatic decision-making of the computer.

Determining Open-to-Buy Dollars

A buying plan is originated every 3, 6, or 12 months, and brought up to date at intervals within these time periods. The plan begins with an estimate of dollars of sales for the next season or specified period. When sales goals have been set, the desired stock levels are determined which will achieve the planned turnover. Then the average purchase markon is decided and estimated markdowns are figured:

A.	Estimated Sales in Department X Over the Next 6 Months	$1,000,000
B.	Planned Annual Turnover	4 times
C.	Planned 6 Months Turnover	2 times
D.	Average Dollar Inventory Level Needed to Achieve 2 Turns in 6 Months	$ 500,000
E.	Purchase Markon (percentage)	40%
F.	Purchase Markon (dollars)	$ 400,000
G.	Anticipated Markdowns (percentage)	1%
H.	Anticipated Markdowns (dollars)	$ 10,000
I.	Planned Net Markon over the next 6 months (F minus H)	$ 390,000

The controller's division and top management then combine the proposed plans of each merchandise division to make sure that the company's overall goals will be achieved. After any necessary changes or adjustments have been made, the buyer is given his final, approved plan which will control his actions for the projected period of time. At weekly or monthly intervals thereafter, he will receive sales, purchase, and markdown figures which he will measure against the plan. When there are important discrepancies, either his plan will be altered or he will change the direction of some of his activities.

It is imperative that the controller place dollar limits on merchandise investment, and the buyer must put aside his rather natural antipathy to the financial division and work cooperatively with it. Each buying-merchandising team must keep within the investment boundaries which the previous experience of the company and of other companies has shown to be reasonable. Management cannot allow a merchandising division to sweep its buying mistakes under the rug and demand more and more dollars to invest. But a balance and flexibility must be arrived at that does not place an overbought merchandising division in a debtors' prison from which there is little chance of escape. Punishment of an over-invested merchandising division by cutting off all further funds will make it increasingly less attractive to customers and lessen its opportunity to work out its problems. Open-to-buy restrictions should not inhibit the merchandising of summer toys because a late, cold spring had prevented a sell-through in apparel. Poor performance in one classification should not prevent ex-

120

ploitation of a sudden fad or the sharp growth of a special category. Control ideally should be by items rather than by dollars. It makes no sense to penalize the buyer for past errors by forcing him to pass up present opportunities. The controller has heavy responsibilities in his financial management of a giant retailing company, but the merchandising divisions should make the final decisions on the flexibility of open-to-buy allotments within the guidelines set up by top management.

TURNOVER

Turnover is the number of times that a classification of merchandise is sold and replenished within a specific period of time. It is measured by the ratio between sales volume for the period and the value of the average inventory carried to supply these sales. For example, suppose annual volume on men's sport shirts in a store is $10,000. If the values of the January 1st beginning inventory and of the December 31st ending inventory were respectively $3,000 and $2,000, then the average value of the two inventories is $2,500. Consequently, the turnover achieved on men's sport shirts for that year is four times: the number of times that the average inventory of $2,500 goes into the annual volume of $10,000.[4]

The importance of good turnover to retailing success can hardly be overestimated. If an outstanding merchant can sell $10,000 worth of men's sport shirts with a turnover of eight times and half the average investment, he obviously has funds available to operate another department and double his profits. If he is borrowing money to finance inventories, turnover improvement will permit him to keep less stock in relation to sales and he will be able to borrow less, thereby saving on interest charges. Good turnover is also a measurement of performance in general. It indicates that the merchandise has been bought and sold properly.

[4]If monthly inventory figures are available, the average inventory for the 12 months will be preferable to the average of only the year-end inventories; in a seasonal line like men's sport shirts, the inventory will have been much higher in May than in December.

Turnover will vary among categories of merchandise. Men's wear doesn't turn as fast as more volatile ladies' wear. House furnishings don't turn as fast as health and beauty aids. Trade figures on what is considered good turnover for a particular category are available to help establish goals. The achievement of these goals means that undesirable goods and odds and ends have not been allowed to accumulate and clutter up store displays, and to restrict the flow of fresh, exciting new merchandise into the stores to stimulate customers and personnel alike. The buyer with good turnover always has open-to-buy because the investment dollars allotted to him are not used up by excessive quantities of slow-moving merchandise. He is, therefore, in a much better position to take advantage of current market opportunities.

Turnover can also be too high; model stocks must be maintained. Turnover figures mean nothing to customers; out-of-stock conditions do. A store with a much higher turnover rate than its competitors, but with an excessive number of customer walk-outs because of out-of-stocks, either has miscalculated in planning its turnover or has balanced its stocks poorly. If a retailer's problem with an overstock of blankets causes him to skimp on the replenishment of a basic item like hand lotion and to be out of it, he will find his hand lotion customers totally unsympathetic. Over-zealous attention to turnover may also lead to smaller, more frequent ordering, with the resulting loss of quantity discounts, and with the creation of additional order-writing, invoice payments, and receiving chores. Like other elements of retail profit, turnover is a function of selling and merchandising, and should be pursued with moderation and flexibility.

There are many things the buyer can do to improve his turnover within these sensible limits. He can study the inventory situation of individual categories, or even items, within his department to determine exactly where overstocked, low-turnover conditions exist. When bad stock conditions are located, he should use his influence to initiate better display, return to supplier, redistribution of goods within his company, or judicious markdowns. He can streamline his assortments even further. He can study the peaks and valleys of demand to keep his stocks in the right proportion to sales. He can use cautious testing procedures in a few stores before plunging deeply into new items and lines. He can quit buying an item before it has slowed down in sales. And he can avoid the ever-present temptation to buy prestige merchandise that far exceeds his usual price points and that does not belong in his stores. Buyers who control their stocks in these ways, and, at the same time, work at the aggressive promotion of wanted merchandise, will always have satisfactory turnover and open-to-buy dollars.

VENDOR DISCOUNTS

Cash Discounts

A cash discount is a financial incentive offered by the vendor so that he will be paid more promptly and, thereby, avoid the costs of employing more money in his business. Clearly, if his customers pay him ten days after the delivery of goods rather than 90 days later, he will have the money 80 days sooner to buy additional raw materials, pay his employees, and so on. On the other hand, if he receives the money in 90 days, he may have to pay to borrow more funds, or be forced to keep a larger amount of cash on hand that could have been used more productively elsewhere.

The cash discount is most commonly 1 or 2 percent for payment within 10 or 30 days, but it may also be zero or 3 or more percent. Discount amounts are usually the same or very similar among vendors in the same industry.

Since a 1 or 2 percent discount for payment within 10 or 30 days is a high rate of interest on an annual basis, it is an important source of net profit for the retailer. It is the responsibility of the buyer to be sure that he is securing the maximum cash discount available and to work with the invoice payments division to have bills paid in time to earn it. A cash discount should be traded for separately, independent of other price negotiations. It should never be sacrificed as a means of consummating a particular deal or for a temporary price advantage.

A less common form of cash discount is given for advance payment or "anticipation." In this case, the vendor allows an additional cash discount for payment before the due date of the invoice. For example, if a 2 percent cash discount is still deductible 30 days after the invoice date, an additional anticipation discount may be allowed if paid in only 10 days. In this case, the vendor has his payment for the purchase in 10 days instead of 30 and allows for an extra discount because he has the use of the money for the 20 additional days.

Trade Discounts

Trade discounts are allowances offered by the vendor to encourage retailers to sell his products. If a manufacturer has produced an item with a projected price tag of $1.00 and is offering it to retailers in general for 60¢, he is giving a trade discount of 40 percent. In common retailing parlance, this 60¢ is referred to as the manufacturer's basic price.

But a vendor will surely prefer to sell to a giant mass merchandiser rather than to one tiny, independent retailer. His dependence on big volume to cover his factory expenses and his selling costs will cause him to seek the advantages of large-scale selling and to offer trade discounts beyond his basic price to secure larger orders. Such trade discounts are of two types: quantity discounts based on the premise that larger orders are more profitable; and advertising and promotional allowances to encourage and reward the retailer who actively helps to sell the product beyond the normal presentation and selling effort. Once the vendor has decided what his schedule of trade discounts should be to provide the maximum inducement to his customers to buy, he is required by law to offer this schedule to all customers equally. These legal requirements will be discussed further later in the book.

Quantity Discounts. A vendor will carefully calculate his discount structures to maximize the economies that larger shipments will bring to his particular company setup. But these discount structures must also be consistent with the retailer's operation, and be so designed that they actually do result in larger orders of a practical, usable quantity for the retailer. Generous allowances for full truckload shipments may be very practical for a manufacturer, but if no retailer can use that much the discount is meaningless.

The intrinsic practicality of many quantity discounts is immediately clear. If freshly manufactured goods are packed and placed in stock for shipments in units of, say, two dozen, and the retailer orders in units of one-half dozen, the costs of repacking are considerable. The manufacturer's price schedule will almost certainly be highest for purchases calling for "broken," repacked cartons. The economies of shipping in larger and larger units, such as master cartons, full pallets, half truckloads, full truckloads and carloads, are sought and shared with retailers through quantity discounts.

Transportation rates have a great effect on discounts. If the minimum shipping rate applies only to quantities that are 200 pounds or larger, the price of shipping less than 200 pounds goes up considerably. Manufacturers commonly quote a minimum invoice amount at which they deliver and pay the transportation; either they refuse to fill orders for less than this amount or they may agree to fill smaller orders at a higher cost to the retailer. They then frequently offer graduated discounts as the invoice amounts increase. If $50 is prepaid without any quantity discount, perhaps an invoice of $250 will receive a quantity allowance of 1 percent, $500 will receive 2 percent, $1,000, 3 percent, and so on. Obviously, manufacturers' quantity discounts are very carefully calculated to yield economies and to sell more merchandise more effectively.

Promotional and Advertising Allowances. Legally, suppliers must offer all retailers the same opportunity to benefit from allowances. But the form and amount of a vendor's allowance will depend on both the overall marketing plan for the product and what is required to compete with other manufacturers for maximum retailer selling support. A manufacturer of a highly advertised toiletries item may offer a temporary 5 or 10 percent discount, or one piece free with each 12 pieces ordered, to ensure complete or larger stocks in stores during a peak advertising period. Or he may prefer to establish an annual 5 percent allowance

125

which would be available for such purposes as cooperative advertising, trading stamp offers, circular distributions, special promotional displays, prizes, guaranteed permanent display space, as well as for combinations of these promotional devices. A housewares manufacturer may be faced with a peak seasonal demand for his products. Perhaps he has the twin problems of getting enough of his merchandise to the point of sale to meet this peak demand, as well as finding sufficient storage space in anticipation of this peak shipping and selling period. His promotional allowances will probably be used to encourage retailers to buy earlier than they otherwise might, thereby relieving both of his problems. Manufacturers of the strongest, most popular items and brands will find it unnecessary to offer anything but the smallest allowance to the retailer to stock and promote their merchandise. The weakest items and brands will carry the most alluring allowances in order to obtain aggressive retailer support.

The buyer must weigh the value of the quantity discount and of the promotional and advertising allowance against the cost of maintaining additional investment. If he orders larger quantities and has no plans to sell them in the same period of time, he has increased his model stock and reduced his turnover. His management will have provided him with guidelines for stock replenishment. For example, taking into consideration such factors as the cost of money invested, delivery schedules, costs of placing individual orders, and storage space available, management may assign the buyer a turnover goal of five times a year in a particular category of merchandise, or a normal stock of about ten weeks. How much should this normal stock be increased to earn a temporary price allowance of, say, 10 percent? What is the optimum order size in this circumstance? [5]

The precise mathematics of this determination will have been handled for the buyer by financial administrators, and, in-

[5]The Economic Order Quantity (EOQ) is treated in full in such texts as Robert G. Brown's *Statistical Forecasting for Inventory Control* (New York: McGraw-Hill Book Company, 1959).

creasingly, by computers, so that he will be given a formula to follow. For example, he may be advised that his stocks should be increased from a 10- to a 15-weeks' supply when a 10 percent allowance is offered. However, this purely financial judgment must be tempered by merchandising considerations. The 10 percent offer may depend on promotional or advertising performance which the buyer may believe is inadvisable or untimely. On the other hand, the 10 percent allowance may contribute to a program which would greatly increase sales, and, therefore, might call for even larger stocks than would normally be sold in 15 weeks.

The supplier is as eager to offer inducements to sell more of his products as the buyer is to receive them. The big chain buyer must be alert to take maximum advantage for his company of quantity discounts as well as of promotional and advertising allowances.

MISCELLANEOUS EXPENSE CONTROL

The buyer must do his share to control all expenses which he affects in his work. Wasteful usage of the various forms of communication, such as the telephone, stenographic service, and postage, can become significant when the cost is multiplied by the total number of buyers. There are always more efficient ways to handle or eliminate clerical and paper work, and the buyer must be alert to recognize them. Travel expenses should be kept under control. Use of staff personnel in such departments as sales promotion, advertising, display, and testing laboratories must fit the importance of the total project.

But facilities and staffs exist because they perform a function and make a contribution to net profit. Percentages are guides, not ends in themselves. If an expense is incurred to do a job that contributes to net profit, it is defensible and should not be cut. The responsible buyer will recognize the interdependence of all personnel and cooperate with management in the control of all expense monies.

8

The Buyer's Role in the Transportation and Warehousing of Merchandise

We manufacture goods with horsepower and then distribute them with manpower. . . . In the interest of overall efficiency, marketing in the years ahead must utilize to a greater degree all helpful technological developments in such areas as the logistics of materials movement, the mechanics of materials handling, automation of warehousing and stock movement, electronic data processing, inventory management, and knowledge of consumer behavior.[1]

George Schwartz, former president of S. H. Kress & Co., tells a story about a top Sears official who stated that although Sears' annual sales were $2.4 billion, the average purchase by a customer was $4.00, and that the problem of making a retailing profit revolved largely around the efficient handling of the 600 million transactions necessary to achieve that sales total.

The typical consumer prefers to buy items one at a time. She seeks maximum value, attractive merchandise, convenience, a pleasant setting, and as much individual attention as she can have—all at the lowest possible price.

The mass merchant is in the dilemma of trying to satisfy all of the consumer's wants while maintaining low distribution costs. If his

[1]Malcolm B. McNair, "Challenge of the 1960's," *Harvard Business Review,* September-October 1961, p. 26.

retail prices are competitive, his costs must be kept low enough to result in a net profit; and he must seek these lower costs through larger-scale purchasing and minimum distribution costs. He would obviously much prefer to sell larger quantities to the consumer than one item at a time.

High on the list of retailing costs is the expense of physically handling and storing merchandise until it is placed within the reach of the customer. Handling refers to the transfer or transport from one point to another; storage covers warehousing. Decisions involving the transportation and warehousing of merchandise will be critical to the resolution of the problem of buying in the largest quantities and selling in the smallest.

THE TRANSPORTATION OF MERCHANDISE

Transportation is a complicated subject requiring a high degree of specialization, and no buyer is likely to know all the quickest and cheapest methods to ship specific merchandise to specific points. But an unwise selection of a transportation routing can wipe out profit. If a buyer who is faced with the prospect of the late arrival of goods for a pre-set promotional date decides to switch from the least expensive, slowest method of transportation to air express, he may reduce the planned markon of 20 percent to zero. What, then, is the buyer's role in determining that his purchases are moved most efficiently?

First, since the buyer does not usually know exact costs and delivery schedules, he must seek this information from specialists in order to plan the timing of his deliveries and to obtain the lowest possible transportation costs.

Second, he must know or find out how the various locations of his stores affect delivery times so that, as far as is possible, he may schedule shipments for simultaneous arrival at all outlets.

Third, his total merchandising plan must provide for delivery at a specific time and for a routing that will be economical enough to yield the planned margin after transportation costs. Faulty scheduling can result in the arrival of special quantities of men's wear the day after Father's Day, of advertised goods the day after the ad appears, or of fast-selling basic goods after the store has been out-of-stock for some time.

Fourth, he must consider transportation as part of his total effort to obtain better turnover with smaller investment. High interest rates and the increased cost of money have forced a more scientific management of inventory and the whittling down of investments. To cite an extreme example, the choice by the buyer or the transportation division of a riverboat barge in order to save in delivery cost per ton mile might add two weeks to the time in transit and, if invoice payments are based on date of shipment, tie up capital for an additional two week period or increase the risks of damage, deterioration, and style obsolescence. On the other hand, riverboat barge transportation costs may be especially low because they are based on unusually large shipments for which a special quantity price was obtained. Of course, these quantity savings must also be weighed against the added burden that the additional dollars put on turnover of investment funds.

The Buyer's Choices

The buyer will often be faced with a choice of items of equal value from different shipping points, which are therefore subject to widely different transportation costs, or he may have to choose between an item on which he pays the freight expense and one on which the vendor has included delivery costs in the price. Or the vendor may offer an item at two prices—one with delivery costs included and one without delivery costs included. If the buyer's stores are clustered near the vendor's shipping point, delivery costs will probably be lower than if the stores are widely scattered at great distances. Since the vendor has based his price including delivery on average delivery costs, the buyer should choose the delivered price when the stores are distant and the undelivered price when they are close at hand.

Most mass merchandisers will consolidate small shipments into large shipments when delivery costs are high in relation to the value of the merchandise. Railroad trucking lines in big shipping centers like New York and Chicago will have consolidation points where they will hold small shipments intended for one destination until they can be combined with others to total an economical size.

All of these choices which the buyer must face involve the weighing of transportation savings against the necessary delay in delivery time. The buyer must be aware of the alternatives open to him and communicate with his transportation division in order to reach the best decisions.

WAREHOUSING

Advantages

From the standpoint of the individual store, the maintenance of complete warehouse stocks makes all items available by regularly scheduled and frequent deliveries. An improved in-stock position is almost certain to be achieved. The warehouse can be set up to break down large, full-case packs into smaller quantities more in line with the store's immediate requirements and turnover goals. The individual store no longer has to decide what is an economical or minimum shipment from each vendor; nor does it have to cope with separate listings of merchandise or order sheets. Moreover, the reordering and replenishment of merchandise from a warehouse are usually reduced to a simple checklist system, a minimum of counting, or to an economical "eyeball" check. Because manufacturers' minimum direct shipments tend to become larger and larger as transportation costs mount, stores are happy to have the opportunity to order in more manageable quantities of individual items through a warehouse. And since most stores are limited in space and operate at a higher rental per square foot than do warehouses, storage is less expensive at warehouses than at stores.

The retailer with warehousing facilities can be assured of a specialized management, as well as mechanized handling of merchandise well beyond the capabilities of the individual store. Many of the newer warehouses, called distribution centers, are huge and highly automated. A giant retailer can tailor the operations of his own warehouses to fit his company's requirements exactly. Deliveries from suppliers to warehouses would obviously be in much larger quantities than to individual stores, and, therefore, would offer the advantages of quantity rates. The economies of shipping in full carloads or truckloads might be available. To avoid the waste of having trucks return empty after delivering to stores, back-hauling shipments can be arranged with manufacturers who deliver to the warehouse. For example, a warehouse truck delivering to stores in the Cleveland area might be scheduled to pick up a load of electric light bulbs from a manufacturer in that area to be brought back to the warehouse in the same truck that otherwise might have returned empty. A series of strategically located warehouses can achieve a regional balance of distribution and delivery on schedule that might otherwise be impossible. Warehousing further offers the advantages of quality control by providing for systematic inspection at a central point before distribution to stores. Processing and ticketing are often done at the warehouse. And, very important, large-scale warehouse operations make the use of a computer, with its great operational advantages, more feasible.

The availability or non-availability of warehousing and its effectiveness in distributing his purchases will be of great daily interest to the buyer. He and his merchandising superiors will constantly study ways to take maximum advantage of the company's warehousing program. Extra-large purchases at very favorable prices may be possible only when the storage capacity of a warehouse is available. Import buying, because it is most often done on a large scale, may be practical only if warehousing space is adequate. A buying decision to stock broader assortments of merchandise may hinge on the availability of a warehousing system that can break down large, economical purchases into smaller shipments that individual stores can handle. Warehousing, then, gives the buyer greater flexibility in his purchasing.

Disadvantages

On the other hand, warehouses and big distribution centers are very expensive, and alternative storage facilities, such as public warehouses, may be available. A rapidly growing company may wish to conserve its capital for more immediately profitable purposes. Individual stores may have adequate storage space that a new warehouse would only duplicate, thereby adding to total rental costs. Stores may be so widely scattered that no warehouse could be central enough to serve them economically. Moreover, the wholesaler stands ready to perform most warehouse functions for a reasonable fee.

In some categories, manufacturers are so eager to control or influence the distribution and merchandising of their products that they willingly perform the warehousing functions without charging the retailer. Suppliers may deliver promptly in minimum quantities and even take over the reordering and display of their items in the stores, making warehousing an unnecessary expense. Also, small-scale, hand-to-mouth buying without warehousing does postpone the ownership of merchandise, thereby conserving capital. For example, the corner druggist who telephones his wholesaler each evening for replacement of that day's sales is surely paying a premium for his merchandise, but his investment is minimal in both merchandise and warehousing facilities. When capital is in short supply, small-scale, higher-cost ordering may be preferable to warehousing and the investment it requires.

Categories of Merchandise Most Suitable to Warehousing

Although the buyer will be committed to a broad, company-wide distribution program beyond his control, he will be able to decide whether or not to warehouse certain categories. One possibility may be to split his purchases between wholesalers and his own warehouse. In the area of health and beauty aids, for example, he would probably choose to warehouse the faster-selling items that his stores can use in full-case quantities. The ease and skill with which items can be handled will often be determining factors in deciding whether or not to warehouse. The rate at which consumer demand draws an item from the warehouse will be even more important. If an item or category moves so slowly that it does not meet the prescribed warehouse turnover rate, perhaps it should be purchased from a wholesaler, if at all.

Basic warehouse stocks should be free of the most volatile, seasonal, and fashionable goods; but there are also warehouses specially designed and operated for the efficient distribution of apparel only. Items with a spotty, localized demand, such as ethnic articles, are not suitable for warehouses; or perhaps they might be restricted to a single warehouse when there are several regional ones. Also, if warehouse management has established that it costs 5 percent of purchases to cover warehousing costs, the buyer will be more reluctant to warehouse lines carrying a zero or 3 percent discount, and more eager to warehouse items that carry a 7 to 10 percent allowance.

Top management will be very concerned about the rapidly increasing expense of all forms of transportation and storage. It will constantly be studying and experimenting with new aids to improve distribution while reducing distribution costs.

The buyer, for his part, must have a clear understanding of his company's distribution policies and the options available to him. Warehouses should be used only after all alternatives have been considered. As traditional procedures for the distribution of merchandise give way to more sophisticated methods that are either quicker or more economical, the buyer must be alert to do his part in gaining these advantages for his company.

WAREHOUSING AND FORCE FEEDING

One of the newer systems to replenish stores' merchandise economically is "force-feeding." By this system each participating store receives automatic, periodic delivery of a predetermined quantity of merchandise. These quantities are determined by analyzing statistics which are recorded by computer as merchandise moves into and out of each store.

Replenishment by force-feeding offers several obvious economies. First it replaces the costly conventional ordering procedures by store personnel that consume so many employee hours. Too, it eliminates the probability that a store will be out of stock from time to time because it deviates from its ordering schedule. Thirdly, it gives the central buyers and merchandisers a much tighter control, not only of the selection of merchandise, but also of the depth in which it is stocked. For example, if the central merchandisers are convinced that a specific quantity of an item is appropriate for a store at a particular season, force-feeding circumvents the possibility that store employees may mistakenly order the item erratically or not at all.

It is clear that an effective force-feeding system would require an efficient central warehousing system. Otherwise, the difficulties of achieving timely delivery of exact, controlled quantities of a wide variety of items from many sources would be enormous. Of course the system also assumes the availability of computer equipment to capture the selling information on which the model shipments would be based.[2]

Since no replenishment system can predict with pin-pointed accuracy the vagaries of customer demand at each store, force-feeding has limitations, but built-in corrective devices help to adjust to these inevitable irregularities. An exception report may be filed by a store after each delivery. This report advises that the automatic delivery quantity is above or below the store's requirements so that the next delivery will fit the store's needs more exactly. However, the economies of the system are undercut if the exceptions filed by store management are frequent and time-consuming.

There are several other problems and limitations of force-feeding. The value of computerized deliveries is impaired if they create frequent overstocks or out-of-stocks. Store display space must be engineered and maintained to have the exact dimensions for the quantity of each item received. It may be necessary to allow space at another location in the store for temporary storage of excess quantities. Packing quantities of items delivered must be small enough to fit the display space they earn.

Provision for seasonal demand and for the sudden increase or decline in popularity of items must also be made. If a Boy Scout troop leader buys every jackknife in the store on a Saturday

[2]It is not surprising, then, that a leading experimenter with force-feeding is McCrory-McClellan-Green, the general merchandise chain with a highly sophisticated warehousing system and a dedication to the use of computers in refining its distribution system. For a detailed report on this company's progress with force-feeding, see "MMG/Evolution of a Revolution," *Chain Store Age,* December 1970, pp. 54-67.

morning, a special order must be made to replenish stock, but, since that sale was unusual, the quantity on the special order should not be included when the store's model delivery is computed. Force-feeding will be most effective for basic merchandise on which customer demand is most stable. It will be least helpful for fad items whose life span is short and unpredictable. Seasonal items like bathing suits and baseball bats cannot be distributed this way.

Since the fixed costs of replenishing a 25¢ item at the store level approximate the costs of reordering a $10 item, the elimination of store ordering of low-priced items will yield the greatest savings in proportion to the value of the merchandise. Thus the appeal of the force-feeding system is greatest for lower-priced merchandise items.

Not only must a strong warehousing system exist to make force-feeding effective, but the central buying team must make the right merchandise selection and engineer it for maximum display space productivity. It must buy so that the right merchandise is always available in the correct quantities at the warehouse. Seasonal fluctuations, if any, must be anticipated. Decisions must be reached when merchandise categories should be added or withdrawn from force-feeding. If exception reports filed by stores indicate that certain items are being delivered in the wrong quantities, corrections must be made quickly. Just as a computer can be only as effective as the program that controls it, distribution systems like force-feeding must depend for success on sound buying decisions. Here the buyer becomes more important than in systems of replenishment based on the judgments of individual stores. A more centralized system brings more centralized buying control and responsibility; and buying decisions made for a large group of stores should be more skilled and more accurate than the hurried decisions of individual store managements.

The development of quicker and better data through computers, and of improved physical handling of merchandise through mechanization, will continue to have their impact. Style is more important than ever and calls for faster distribution methods. And pressures for the better use of capital demand speedier deliveries and smaller investments. Continuing experiments to reduce the heavy expenses of distribution—to substitute horsepower for manpower, and the computer for individual arithmetic—depend heavily on two things. First, a warehousing system must exist which can make little shipments out of big shipments efficiently and, second, the buying organization must be capable of effectively developing and controlling the system.

9

The Buyer's Role in
Display and Sales Promotion

. . . When you ask your buyer: What did you do today that's different from what your competing counterpart is doing?, he must have an answer—at least a reasonable percentage of the time. Impossible on every item. Impossible 100% down the line. But truly possible more times than casually greets the eye. [1]

In the quest for profits, the ultimate goal of all retail personnel is the continuous production of traffic at the point of sale. Achievement of this goal requires not only the right merchandise at the right price, but also the right display and sales promotion. The buyer's role in display and sales promotion will vary greatly among different types of retail organizations. The department store buyer is usually very active at the point of sale and knows intimately how his merchandise is being presented to the customer. The mass-merchandise buyer, on the other hand, is far removed from the point of sale and, except for his occasional visits to the store, must rely almost completely on other personnel to sell what he has bought.

Merchandise selections in many categories are so standardized by dominant manufacturers and their national advertising that

[1]Abe Jacobsen, "On Sales Promotion," *The Discount Merchandiser,* October 1968, p. 36.

stocks are nearly identical in competitive stores. A store's success in selling merchandise categories of these standardized types is not based so much on its buying skills as on its ability to attract and sell to customers. Although this fact tends to reduce the importance of the purchasing or procurement part of the buying role, it will emphasize to the buyer the need for maximum involvement in the display and promotion of his merchandise.

In small companies, the full responsibility for display, promotion, advertising, testing, comparison shopping, fashion forecasting, and statistical analysis may be assumed by the line organization of the merchandising division. This line organization is the chain of authority—consisting generally of a general merchandise manager, divisional merchandise managers, buyers, and assistant buyers—through which authority flows in a direct and clear line.

The larger the sales volume of a chain, the more likely the chain is to assign these promotion and sales functions to staff personnel—specialists who are experts in their fields and are free to concentrate on their specialties. These specialists perform their staff functions for the line organization. Because of their semi-detachment from any particular merchandise department, these staff people will be able to put together balanced programs in their areas for the entire company.

The great importance of coordination, communication, and cooperation between line and staff personnel is obvious. However, some degree of friction between the two groups is probably inevitable. Rare is the buyer who does not feel he is being short changed in his share of promotional and advertising monies, or in the space and selling attention his categories are receiving at the point of sale. Lines of authority are not always clearly defined, and general merchandise managers often spend valuable time resolving conflicts between the two groups.

Staff people often complain, with some justification, that buyers and merchandise managers act in their own selfish interests and exert as much pressure as possible for preference for their departments in display and promotion. Staff people see themselves as the defenders of the store's or company's image against the offbeat, cheapening, or over-aggressive techniques of the line people. They are also likely to be more creative and innovative than the average line-organization man and to feel that the buyer and merchandise manager who resist their ideas lack imagination.

But Theodore Levitt, a member of the Harvard Business School faculty and author of an article entitled "Creativity Is Not Enough," defends the position of the line manager and buyer. He writes:

> The trouble with much of the advice that business is getting today about the need to be more vigorously creative is, essentially, that its advocates have generally failed to distinguish between the relatively easy process of being creative in the abstract and the infinitely more difficult process of being innovationist in the concrete. . . . Their emphasis is almost all on the thoughts themselves. . . . So-called creative people often (though certainly not always) pass off on others the responsibility for getting down to brass tacks. They have plenty of ideas but little business-like follow-through.[2]

It is interesting to note how the G. C. Murphy Co. handles the cumbersome problem of communication between its buyers and the sales planning committee. A few buyer supervisors at Murphy (or a few divisional merchandise managers in companies that do not have buyer supervisors) present suggested special merchandise to the sales planning committee. After the basic promotional decisions and choices have been made by the planning committee, the individual buyers are called in to work out the remaining problems and details with members of the sales promotion division: "No committee meeting could possibly cover all of the details needed to make a promotion flow smoothly. So after each meeting a liaison team unique to Murphy, picks up the ball. . . . Three sales promotion coordinators work directly with the buyers to iron out all the detail work. One coordinator . . . to each merchandising division . . . selects the supplementary promotional items, pinpoints the facts needed in signwork, roughs out suggested displays,

[2]Theodore Levitt, "Creativity Is Not Enough," *Harvard Business Review*, May-June 1963, pp. 72-73.

etc." [3] In this fashion, the buyer is given an opportunity to fulfill his specialist role and to participate in the vitally important function of sales promotion while overall efficiency and cooperation are maintained.

Suffice it to say that much honest difference of opinion is inevitable between line and staff personnel. Blessed is the retail organization that can resolve these differences and receive the benefits of both groups working together.

MERCHANDISE DISPLAY

Merchandise display refers to the location or the amount of space a category or an individual item receives in a store of a particular size. A good example of the interaction of merchandise assortments, model stocks and display layouts is provided by the J. J. Newberry Company's continuing experiment called "Modular Planning." [4] Modular planning endeavors to:

Measure the market opportunity for a classification of merchandise.
Set up the minimal assortment of goods that will achieve maximum sales by category of merchandise.
Set up minimal inventory by item that will be sufficient to get these sales without excess stocks.
Set up a model stock display or display modules. (This means the actual construction of a model store display of the exact quantity of each item that will achieve the above totals in proportion to the contribution a specific category makes to the store's total sales and profits.)

It is interesting to note that Newberry moved its buyers into the Long Branch store where this project was being carried out. The buyers built the model displays for the merchandise categories they purchased, and received a practical education in the effective use of display space and the importance of assortment control.

3"Murphy on the Move/Sales," *Chain Store Age,* December 1967, p. 142.

4"What's Behind Newberry's Long Branch Project? " *Chain Store Age,* March 1968, pp. 32-34.

141

Display as a Selling Tool for the Buyer

The value of an attractive presentation of merchandise to customers is self-evident. In some high-priced fashion areas it is an art. In the more prosaic areas, display presents more of a problem in arithmetic—the problem of dividing display footage into categories that will produce maximum sales and profits.

An effective display enhances the appeal of the product at the point of sale; takes advantage of existing store traffic without the extra cost of advertising to attract more; and provides new interest to the buying public as well as to the selling staff. A minor rearrangement of a display will sometimes give a fresh, more interesting look to a merchandise grouping or to an entire department.

The store's design, ceilings, wall decor, lighting, carpeting, and fixturing are all part of an established image to which the buyer must adapt his contribution to display. His recommendations regarding the use of point-of-purchase display pieces furnished by manufacturers must conform to the general atmosphere of the store. He should not suggest a hashed-out display of mill-end seconds in a carpeted, softly-lighted area devoted to high fashion wear. Customers have a definite idea of how a store should look to support the character of its merchandise and its general price appeal. This image will determine whether or not to increase the use of mannequins, add aisle space, introduce more carpeting, cover exposed cinder block, and so on.

It is also extremely important to analyze the use of each square foot of display space for maximum production of sales and profit. Once the listings of merchandise have been honed to offer the best assortments in the right proportion, store management will need the most detailed guidance in the presentation of the merchandise to the customers.

The Plan-O-Gram

A plan-o-gram is a detailed diagram which shows the exact placement of each item within a fixed display area. In most cases it will also show the exact amount of the item to be displayed.

142

For basic, staple merchandise displayed on wall shelving or on the gondola fixturing used in all mass-merchandising outlets, but most familiarly in supermarkets, the plan-o-gram becomes a precise blueprint. Because statistics are usually available in great detail, either from all stores within a company or from the industry as a whole, the determination of the correct display space for an item is relatively easy. Periodic revisions in the plan-o-gram will maintain an accurate balance between demand and display which will be applicable to every store in the company. Once or twice a year will probably be frequent enough in a category like school supplies, for example, to send stores an up-to-date plan-o-gram reflecting the growth of one item and the decline of another, or perhaps the addition of a private brand item.

Of course, there will be variations in demand between stores, but these differences are more likely than not to be exaggerated by local management. The desire to excel and take advantage of a special demand is laudable, but it will usually be found that the opportunity for extra sales is out of proportion to the special effort required, and that there will be at least as many other sales opportunities missed within the plan-o-gram program in the same store. Preplanned display programs are usually accurate and reliable, and they free store management's time for other productive pursuits. The manager who wants to change and second guess the buyer's plan-o-gram may well be perpetuating his own merchandising biases and errors and missing the opportunity to move into new developments and opportunities that only buying and display specialists can uncover for him.

The buyer will probably have an important role in setting up model displays. Because of his closeness to current and future market developments, he will certainly be consulted when revisions are needed. His decisions on assortment changes will be immediately reflected to some degree in display changes. He will constantly be seeking a more favorable exposure in interior and window promotional display space for his particular lines.

To illustrate the use of plan-o-grams, two simple examples will serve. The first example, shown in Figure 1, demonstrates how a buyer might allocate his space to sewing notions. Let us assume his

143

FIGURE 1   Plan-o-gram for Display of Sewing Notions

Percent of space allotted to sewing lines today									
21.9% buttons	15.7% thread	15.6% zippers	2.1% needles	2.7% scissors	7.4% patches	15.2% trims and bindings	6.8% elastics	12.6% sewing aids

←──────────────── 22 ft. 8 in. ────────────────→

management has assigned him 22 feet and 8 inches of floor space. From current sales statistics, supplemented by industry information about trends, the buyer will determine the percentage of that footage to be assigned to each category of sewing notions—to buttons, threads, zippers, etc. [5]

Once the total amount of footage for each classification of sewing notions has been assigned, the next step is to further refine the plan-o-gram to allocate space for individual items. For example, in the plan-o-gram in Figure 1 buttons have been allocated 21.9 percent, or 5 feet, of the total space. If our assigned display fixture is four feet from top to bottom, the buyer has a 4' x 5' area in which to merchandise his button assortment. If this space will hold 30 rows of buttons across and 10 from top to bottom, a total of 300 different buttons can be given separate spaces.

The buyer will then proceed to make selections to fill these spaces, weighing the various variables and trying to strike a balance between variety and salability:

Material: pearl, metal, plastic, wood.
Style: round, square, flat, ball, filigree, novelty.
Color: pearl buttons are mostly white or smoke; metal are usually gold or silver; wood buttons are made in several natural shades and plastics are popular in many colors.

[5]"Sewing Notions on the Counters—Where the Space Is Going," *Chain Store Age, Notions Manugide Section,* August 1969, p. 10.

144

Size: the range is from small shirt buttons or baby buttons to large overcoat buttons.

Season and Store Location: in the winter season or cold weather country more coat and suit buttons will be required; summer will call for more light color buttons. The plan-o-gram will need to be updated at least twice a year in anticipation of the change of seasons.

When the assortment breakdown has been determined the plan-o-gram can be completed in greater detail, as shown in Figure 2.

The selling experience and sales records of both the manufacturer and the retailer will then determine the final breakdown of individual items in each row. Some spaces will be reserved for remainders of discontinued items to be sold out. Some will be reserved for new developments during the life of the plan-o-gram. Some items may be so outstandingly popular that they will be assigned more than one space.

Product Profitability Plans

The construction of the plan-o-gram for buttons may not have taken into account a number of factors bearing on final net profit: markon is usually higher on some items and types of items than on others; some items may require more handling than others or be more perishable; some will deserve a higher space or storage charge because of size, shape or packing. Obviously, a plan-o-gram which came closer to reflecting net profitability rather than just gross sales would be highly desirable. The deterrent to the development of these more valuable plan-o-grams has been the cost of accumulating and applying the additional facts. But it is being done in some areas and turning up some very enlightening information.

Consider the statistics in Figure 3, compiled from a study made of the productivity of 16 different dry dog foods in a chain of supermarkets:

The grocery plan-o-gram in Figure 3 considers handling costs, space costs, and actual gross margin in determining productivity per item, which it calls "yield per exposure foot." Since the yields from individual items in this study range from a loss of 70¢ per foot

145

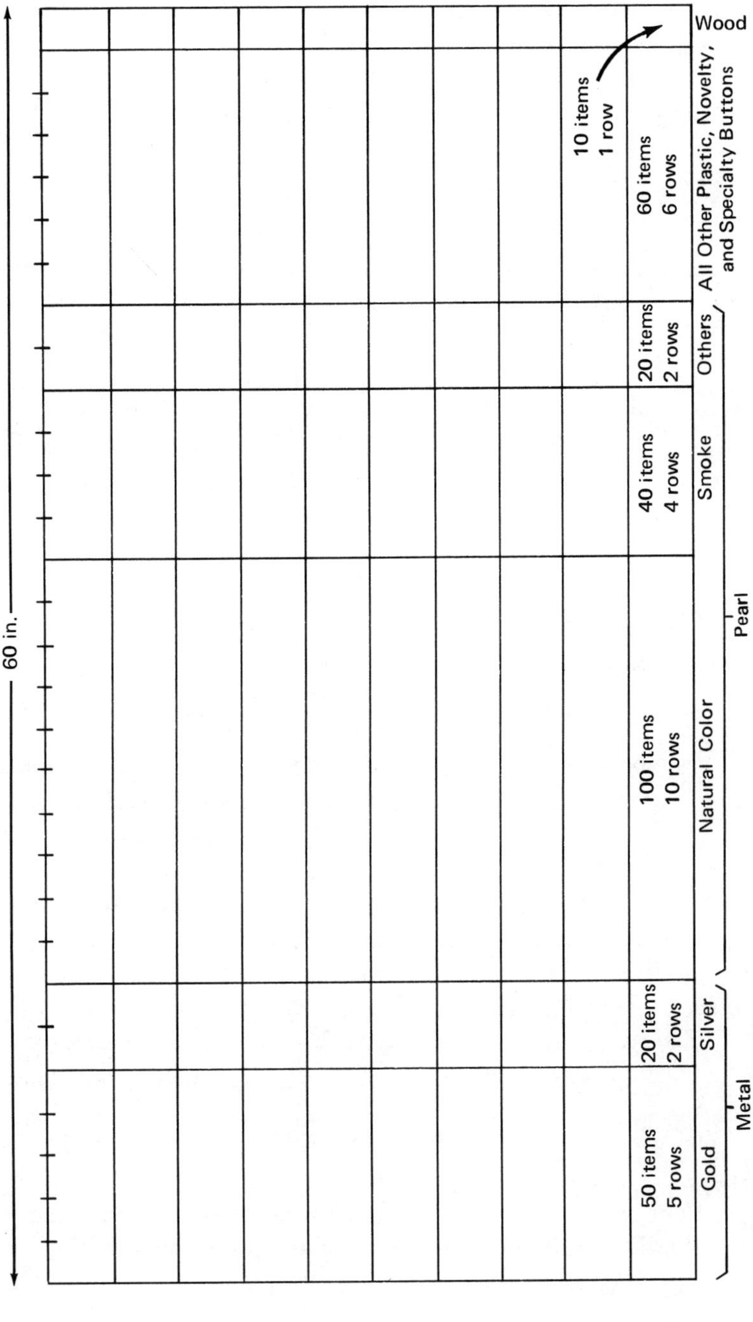

FIGURE 2   Plan-o-gram for Button Category of Sewing Notions

to a gain of $1.57 per foot, and six of the 16 items show losses, it is clear that this analysis would have had great value to the grocery chain management and its buyer in revealing weak points in space allocation. If the space and handling costs have been accurately computed for this plan, the space has been utilized in a very haphazard manner or retail prices have been set erratically and in many instances gross margins are too high or low.

The grocery category selected as an example of a plan-o-gram which reflects profitability could scarcely be more staple or better suited to a mathematical examination of this type. Demand for dry dog food is steady, shifts in the popularity of specific items are not sudden, and fixturing and display for various items are simple and comparable. But the potential value of this type of plan-o-gram and the analysis that goes into its construction is clearly great for other product categories as well. The development of computer assistance in assembling and presenting facts on the profit yield of space will undoubtedly lead to much greater use of this technique in the future by the giant merchandising chains.

Vendors' Point-of-Purchase Display Pieces

Buyers are frequently offered by vendors point-of-purchase displayers which may present an item or category very effectively. Too often, however, these pieces are the creations of advertising agencies who make them too large and elaborate. Carried away by the desire to sell a promotional idea to a vendor, agencies and their art departments sometimes confuse size with effectiveness and the resulting display is impractical for all but the very largest stores with no height, width, and space restrictions. Buyers tend to accept expensive displayers because they are free, with full knowledge that their use will be limited to a small percentage of outlets and for a very circumscribed period of time. A more modest-sized displayer that fits in with overall display principles and is in proportion to the importance of the category is preferable.

Prefabricated Racks

As wage costs continue to mount and the salesclerk continues to

FIGURE 3   Sales Productivity of Dry Dog Food

BRAND	SIZE	PACK	CASE GROSS MARGIN	CASES SOLD	ACTUAL HANDLING COST	SPACE COST	ACTUAL GROSS MARGIN	LESS TOTAL COSTS	TOTAL YIELD	NUMBER SQ. FT. USED	YIELD PER EXPOSURE FOOT
M[1]	2	12	$1.04	0.51	$0.20	$0.16	$0.53	$0.36	$0.17	1.6	$0.11
M[2]	5 lb	10	1.34	0.42	0.17	0.19	0.56	0.36	0.20	1.9	0.11
N[1]	2	12	0.74	0.51	0.20	0.19	0.38	0.39	−0.01	1.9	−0.02
N[2]	5 lb	10	0.94	0.53	0.21	0.20	0.50	0.41	0.09	2.0	0.05
N[3]	25 lb	2	1.48	0.36	0.14	0.18	0.53	0.32	0.21	1.8	0.12
O[1]	26	12	0.80	0.38	0.15	0.21	0.30	0.36	−0.06	2.1	−0.12
O[2]	5 lb	8	0.84	0.32	0.13	0.20	0.27	0.33	−0.06	2.0	−0.12
P[1]	4 lb	12	1.58	0.40	0.16	0.09	0.63	0.25	0.38	0.9	0.42
P[2]	4 lb	10	0.67	0.34	0.14	0.07	0.23	0.21	0.02	0.7	0.03
Q[1]	2	12	0.73	0.24	0.10	0.27	0.18	0.37	−0.19	2.7	−0.70
Q[2]	10 lb	4	0.55	0.20	0.08	0.20	0.11	0.28	−0.17	2.0	−0.34
R[1]	2 lb	12	0.78	0.60	0.24	0.22	0.47	0.46	0.01	2.2	0.01
R[2]	5 lb	10	1.34	0.78	0.31	0.19	1.05	0.50	0.55	1.9	0.29
R[3]	25 lb	2	0.98	0.14	0.06	0.29	0.14	0.35	−0.21	2.9	−0.07
S[1]	18	24	2.20	0.83	0.33	0.09	1.83	0.42	1.41	0.9	1.57
S[2]	36	12	2.10	1.08	0.43	0.12	2.27	0.55	1.72	1.2	1.43
				7.64				$4.06		28.7	$0.14 Avg.

Source: "Space Yield Findings on Pet Foods," *Chain Store Age, Supermarket Executive Edition*, April 1964, pp. 91-95.

disappear from the mass-merchandising scene, the importance of prefabricated displayers will grow. These serve a double purpose. First, they guarantee a uniformity of presentation which both enhances the appearance of the product and helps to control the merchandise assortment and its depth, thereby calling for a minimum of effort and thought at the point of sale. Second, as complete and partial self-service take over, the design of the displayer can perform more of the selling function by effective illustration which may tie in with advertising copy in various media, and by stating the product's main selling points.

One of the problems with prefabricated racks is how to achieve flexibility in stores of varying sizes. Here, too, the manufacturer may think too big, and the resulting rack may well be twice as large as it should be for the smaller stores. It is sometimes possible to construct a two- or three-section rack and assign only one or two sections to the smaller stores. Or manufacturers may be forced to make very different racks for different stores in order to cooperate with the buyer's assortment and model stock plans. In conjunction with his display division, the buyer must take full advantage of these "silent salesmen," but he must control their size so that they will be in proportion to the sales potential.

Fashion and Inter-Department Displays

The display problem is also complicated by the need to present fashion tastefully and attractively to the customer. The lowest-priced goods are decreasing in popularity in our affluent society, and merchants are eager for the higher ticket that fashion brings. But fashion success means more expensive fixturing, better lighting, and personnel who know how to handle and display the merchandise. Timing becomes vitally important and more frequent changes of display must be made. Styles can "drop dead" fast and new fads develop just as quickly. Fashion brings problems as well as opportunities to merchandise display.

A smaller but growing display problem is the spread of "shop" and "boutique" type merchandising to mass merchandisers. The department store's "cruise shop" has its counterparts, and they cross department and classification lines in such a way as to involve several buyers and require special display attention and treatment. But the trend to display goods to attract and appeal to the customer must prevail over the artificial restrictions of classification merchandising. The merchandise content of departments will become less and less rigid in the future and buyers who are aggressively seeking greater sales will tend to cross classification lines. But because these buyers will be entering areas where they are less expert, they will require extra cooperation from the staff specialists in the display and promotion departments, as well as from other buying divisions.

The wise buyer will work closely with his display division and recognize how it contributes to the best possible presentation of the assortments and model stocks that he has so painstakingly assembled. The buyer must also be able to evaluate and make the best use of vendor display materials and selling aids that are available to him in increasing abundance. And he must be quick to advise and assist in the adjustment of display models as the new develops and the old recedes.

SALES PROMOTION

The buyer must not only know his market, buy the right merchandise at the right price, and display it effectively, but he must also be an aggressive promoter of his purchases in cooperation with his sales promotion department. Sales promotion covers every phase of the retail operation that contributes to selling, including advertising, publicity of all kinds, sales training, and credit promotion. Along with merchandise managers, the sales promotion department may be the originator of the company's basic promotion schedule, which will help determine what and when the buyer buys. Promotional merchandise, or merchandise bought with a special appeal beyond that of regular, staple goods, may constitute half the volume or more of some mass merchandisers. Even companies that handle primarily basic goods need sales promotion to build traffic and add excitement to the stores. Since so many categories of merchandise are similar or even identical in competitive stores, promotion becomes the difference—the decisive factor that distinguishes the store that pulls the most customers and volume.

But how often can profit be sacrificed to pull traffic and how deeply can prices be cut and still average out at a satisfactory markon? How can a promotion that is different enough from what the competition is doing to build customer interest be found and traded for? How much of a buyer's restricted advertising budget should be invested in a particular promotion and in what advertising form among those available? Is the store in a high-rent area where foot traffic is heavy, or in a low-rent area where strong advertising and price appeal are necessary to create activity? The buyer will not be able to answer these questions alone, but will have to depend on the skill with which the sales promotion department and top management resolve them. However, as the closest contact with his particular segment of the market, he should do his part to feed facts to his merchandise manager and to the promotional staff.

Every merchant dreams of a carefully planned, integrated sales promotion package with exciting, attractively priced merchandise that is delivered on schedule with well-executed signing, advertising, and display. This dream promotion will certainly succeed at drawing heavy traffic to the store and enabling it to sell large quantities of its everyday, basic lines of merchandise at their regular but higher markons than the promotional goods. It takes skill and cooperation to make this dream a reality, and the buyer's role is central.

There is no greater indicator of the ability and quality of a retail organization than its sales promotion performance. Individual promotional skills must be combined with a high level of cooperation and communication. Even the best retailers have occasionally blushed while advertising ran without the merchandise in the stores; while a well-planned and well-executed promotional program foundered because the merchandise was shoddy or over-priced; or while the store's selling organization failed to execute the well-laid plans. The rewards of good sales promotion are very high but the pitfalls are many.

Advertising

Figures 4 and 5 show the dominance of advertising in the

151

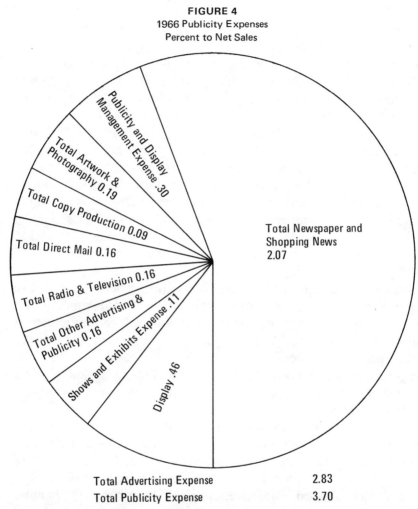

FIGURE 4
1966 Publicity Expenses
Percent to Net Sales

Publicity and Display
Management Expense .30

Total Artwork &
Photography 0.19

Total Copy Production 0.09

Total Direct Mail 0.16

Total Radio & Television 0.16

Total Other Advertising &
Publicity 0.16

Shows and Exhibits Expense .11

Display .46

Total Newspaper and
Shopping News
2.07

Total Advertising Expense	2.83
Total Publicity Expense	3.70

Based on Monthly Retail Trade Statistics, (Table 1), U.S. Department of Commerce, Washington, D.C. and compiled with the Controllers' Congress, NRMA.

Source: *Variety Department Store Merchandiser,* National Retail Merchants Association, April 1968.

Display and Sales Promotion

FIGURE 5

Percentage of Total 1967 Advertising and Promotional Budget Spent on:

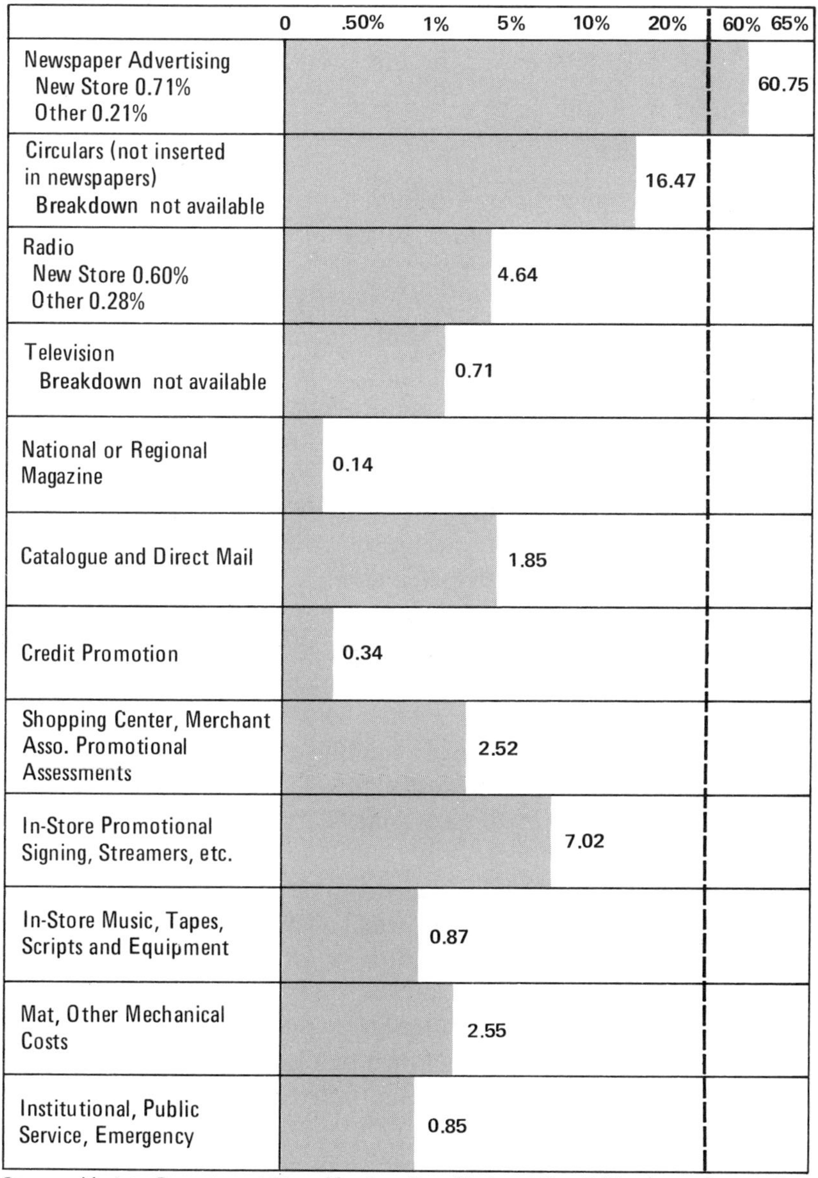

	0	.50%	1%	5%	10%	20%	60% 65%
Newspaper Advertising New Store 0.71% Other 0.21%							60.75
Circulars (not inserted in newspapers) Breakdown not available						16.47	
Radio New Store 0.60% Other 0.28%				4.64			
Television Breakdown not available			0.71				
National or Regional Magazine		0.14					
Catalogue and Direct Mail			1.85				
Credit Promotion		0.34					
Shopping Center, Merchant Asso. Promotional Assessments			2.52				
In-Store Promotional Signing, Streamers, etc.			7.02				
In-Store Music, Tapes, Scripts and Equipment		0.87					
Mat, Other Mechanical Costs			2.55				
Institutional, Public Service, Emergency		0.85					

Source: *Variety Department Store Merchandiser,* National Retail Merchants Association, April, 1968.

promotional expense picture. Figure 4 shows that in 1966, advertising took 2.83 percent of every sales dollar out of a total of 3.70 percent expended for publicity of all kinds. Figure 5 shows the breakdown of the promotional dollar in variety store companies only. Here, over 60 percent of the promotional monies was expended for newspaper advertising, and newspaper and circular advertising together represented over 75 percent of total expenditures.

Whether the advertising medium is print, radio, or television, certain principles will prevail. The layout and copy will have been determined by the character of the store and its merchandise—high-priced or low-priced, fashion or staple. The store's character will also determine if the ad's main intention is to reinforce the image of the entire store in the minds of its customers, with the sale of the particular advertised article a secondary consideration; this is referred to as institutional advertising. In mass merchandising, a factual, hard-hitting, direct approach is much more common than institutional advertising, though top management will always want its advertising to build a specific total impression. The buyer's contribution to effective advertising must fit into the guidelines established for his particular company.

The following list of "do's and don'ts" for the buyer will apply no matter how the advertising dollar is spent:

Do recommend for advertising the biggest volume, top sellers in each classification. *Don't* suggest items of small demand that can't possibly interest one in ten customers.

Do repeat promotions and advertising of proven successes. *Don't* be lured into ads of offbeat, off-brand merchandise because of its novelty.

Do stick to the store's popular price points. *Don't* confuse the clientele by aiming much higher or much lower than what the store stands for in the eyes of the community.

Do promote profitable merchandise in ads as much as possible.

154

Don't consider the price that eliminates profit the only effective advertising tool.

Do be as helpful as possible in supply factual information that will lead to effective follow-through at the point of sale by strong display, signing, and cooperative store involvement. *Don't* do the minimum and hope others will carry the ball the rest of the way.

Do take a leading role in copy preparation as the person closest to the merchandise and best able to appreciate its merits. *Don't* leave the selection of selling points and illustrations to a comparatively uninformed copywriter and expect the best results.

Do cooperate fully with the advertising department, especially in meeting deadlines. *Don't* expect to receive the full benefits of its services without extending the necessary ammunition and enthusiasm.

Do have a point to each advertisement—really have something to sell. *Don't* half-heartedly offer ordinary values and items just to use up an allotted share of an advertising budget.

Do select merchandise for advertising that will do the primary job of creating store traffic and happy customers. *Don't* select items to be advertised just to obtain vendors' promotional allowances. This practice may help the budget slightly but not the net results. Vendor cooperative allowances for slow-moving items are a snare and a delusion.

The breakdown of advertising monies, as shown in Figures 4 and 5, will certainly change in the future as results are scrutinized and new techniques developed. Moreover, total advertising expenditures will no doubt increase. Chains can no longer rely on their central downtown locations to create massive foot traffic without advertising. Outlying, lower-rent stores must use a good deal of advertising to draw customers from other competitive trading centers.

New advertising techniques that will challenge retailers in the future and also involve the buyer include home-to-store shopping by television-telephone, community-antenna TV, new television channels, special audience radio stations, regional editions of magazines and newspapers, and new direct mail methods. As technological development brings these methods within the range of advertising expense budgets, store managements will exploit them and they will become another promotional tool for the buying-merchandising team.

Item Promotion

An obvious and important form of sales promotion is the finding, development, and exploitation of individual fast-selling items. One part of an assortment may unexpectedly blossom into an outstanding seller overnight. Or a winner may be discovered by a vendor who passes the information on to the buyer; or it may be spotted in a competitive store, or in a specialty shop at a price that can be lowered appreciably through mass-merchandising methods.

The first requirement for the successful promotion of items is to spot them quickly. To accomplish this, good and quick means of communication are necessary. A wise buyer will take great care to establish close relationships with the leaders of his industry, with staff personnel in his own company including shoppers and fashion forecasters, and with key personnel at the point of sale. The alert buyer will have identified important store employees and will have set up a feedback procedure to insure a good flow of information. He may have discovered a sales person or department supervisor in a particular store who has an unusual grasp of the merchandise and its selling possibilities. An occasional phone call to this person may prove invaluable in reaching the right decision. Such channels of information contribute significantly to the location of fresh, exciting selling opportunities quickly and ahead of competition.

A truly satisfying and rewarding form of item merchandising is the promotion of the old favorite—the popular item in strong demand season after season. It may be a specialty of that particular company, a private brand, or a product protected by a franchise and therefore not subject to deep price-cutting. Items of this sort usually have a broad market and are frequently repurchased and replaced by the customer; for example, bed sheets or facial tissues. Where store records indicate such long-range popularity and such assured success and profit, productive promotion can be planned well in advance to give the buyer plenty of time to search the market and trade for the most favorable quality and price.

Price Promotion

There is probably no problem more resistant to a formula solution than the pricing of promotional merchandise. Possibilities run the gamut from full markon to selling below cost, and the buyer must be aware of the advantages and disadvantages of each of these solutions. The buying-merchandising team and the sales promotion division must reach their pricing decisions after a careful consideration of the following questions: What price is needed to draw customers to the store? What price is required to move the planned quantity within the sales period? How will the profit from this promotion fit into and affect the store's overall markon budget? At what price is competition selling the item? Can any better price or promotional allowance be secured from the manufacturer that will make sharper pricing possible? Is it the type of item that customers will immediately identify as a bargain, or would they purchase it just as readily at less of a profit sacrifice? Does the company's image, rental, and fixturing recommend or permit pricing on a level with low-rent, minimum-fixturing competitors? And just how important is it right now for the company to show a sales improvement, even if overall markon suffers slightly? (There may be times when top management will wish to assign special priority to sales at the expense of profit.)

Since many of these questions can only be answered tentatively, with inexact measurements, wasteful mistakes are inevitable. By relying on facts, experience, good communication, and measured results, insofar as these are available, such mistakes will be held to a minimum.

157

Promotion of Closeouts

No promotion is likely to be more successful than a genuine housecleaning by a manufacturer of a known, quality item because he wants some quick cash or has made a change in product design or ingredients. The appeal to customers is strong and immediate, and the mass-merchandise buyer dreams of finding such opportunities to use as "door-busting" attractions. Unfortunately, these bonanzas are few and far between.

Profits from a high percentage of closeout purchases are illusory. The cream sells quickly, creating extra sales. But a closeout is a closeout because it is an unbalanced assortment. When the cream is gone, the out-sizes, the wrong colors, the less attractive patterns, and the little-used designs remain—and sales slow to a crawl.

Suppose a buyer purchases and distributes 1,000 "gidgets" which formerly sold for $2.00. They cost 60¢ a piece and are now displayed at $1.00, half the original retail price. Let us assume that the initial response is good and that 800 are sold in a short period of time. The store manager is pleased with the extra sales and the buyer takes pride in his purchase. But it is very likely that, long after the buyer has forgotten the incident, the remaining 200 pieces have had to be further reduced to 50¢ each lest they occupy valuable selling space for too long a period of time. This late markdown will reduce the overall markup on the closeout purchase to 24 percent, and, unless the price reduction was made promptly, it is probably that the store's display space was unproductive for a while. It is always tempting but often unrealistic to yield to the appeal of a sales shot-in-the arm without planning ahead for the clearance of the odds-and-ends remainders. Buyers must accept their responsibility for purchasing only the sort of merchandise that will yield an acceptable profit after every piece has been sold.

Other Forms of Sales Promotion

Enterprising promotion staffs will have a variety of other methods for stimulating sales. Customers may be offered premiums, coupons, or drawings for valuable prizes such as automobiles or trips to Las Vegas. Store-opening extravaganzas may combine several techniques in an all-out effort to attract customers to a new location.

Within the company various incentives are also used to stimulate salespeople as well as store managers and their district managers. Commissions, awards, prizes, and contests are all important promotional tools. The buyer will be offered many such opportunities by vendors seeking preferential effort at the store level. It will be up to him to weigh the supervisory and bookkeeping costs of these special promotions against their potential sales results. W. C. Shaw, Jr., sales vice president of the G. C. Murphy Co., a firm noted for its strong sales promotion department, observed, "These incentives are of such interest that they inspire the weakest link in a store's organization in all-out effort at production. They create a competitive sales atmosphere day-after-day that more nearly approaches sales peaks."[6]

Whatever the devices used and however they are implemented, successful sales promotion requires the intelligent and enthusiastic cooperation of the buyer in achieving a regular program that will provide the store manager with an aggressive plan so complete, so well-timed, and so skillful that it will leave him free to concentrate on selling. Outstanding sales promotion is likely to be characteristic of a whole company rather than of just one of its parts because the right overall climate has been established for aggressive activity. It requires a strong, integrated top-management team that can resist over-restrictive operational and budgetary considerations in favor of the more free-wheeling, chance-taking, and comparatively risky challenges of sales promotion.

[6] "Murphy on the Move/Sales," *Chain Store Age*, December 1967, p. 138.

10

The Buyer and Importing

We deal with about 50 different countries, with the bulk of our business being done through the mail to the various trade offices and companies with which we have established contacts around the world. We have four offices which are staffed by our own employees. These employees are not Americans, but nationals of the countries in which they reside. Their basic job, aside from maintaining the contacts, is to work out product line ideas, screen merchandise, come up with new products, bird-dog shipments, and act as our eyes and ears in the territories they cover.

We make about three buying trips annually, which generally take about two months to plan and last up to ten days at a stretch. Ten days may not sound like a lot but to give you an idea how business is conducted, on a recent trip we spent one day in Taiwan. . . . We had a map of Taipei, the major city, and on the map each company was listed geographically. We hired a driver and interpreter and set a time limit for each interview. We were able to meet our own requirements and come up with major sources that we could maintain on a yearly program. . . . It is a tedious process. But it is the only way we can conduct our business properly.[1]

The above excerpt from an interview with Bernard Field and Richard Hadel, respectively president and general manager of The Akron, a chain of 16 stores in Los Angeles, provides some im-

[1]*Discount Merchandiser,* October 1970, pp. 45-46.

portant insights into the practical working problems associated with direct importing. But the rewards of direct importing are great and other successful direct importers have even reached the point where they are applying mass-merchandising methods to the retailing of imported lines exclusively, in stores specifically designed for that purpose.

IMPORT BUYING

The figures in Tables 1 and 2 on the growth of United States importing clearly indicate its rising importance to retailers.

TABLE 1. Index of United States General Imports—Value of Finished Manufactures (1957-1959=100).

1963	151.5	1967	310.9
1964	174.9	1968	401.2
1965	210.6	1969	474.3
1966	277.3		

Source: U.S. Department of Commerce, *Overseas Business Reports, March 1970,* Table 4, p. 4.

Since the increases took place during years of spectacular growth by most mass merchandisers, especially discounters, it is safe to say that direct importing contributed more than its share to this upsurge.

A mass-merchandise buyer who has been paying $10 for an item from an importer or a domestic manufacturer might be able to get the same item for $8.00 by importing it directly, without using the services of a middleman. And if $1.00 of the $2.00 difference will cover all costs of direct importing, the remaining dollar will be clear profit. In retailing operations, where net profits are often measured in pennies, such a prospect is very exciting. If the retail price of the item is assumed to be $18 and the normal rate of net profit of this mass merchandiser is 5 percent, he will have made 90¢ per item ($18 x 5%) by importing indirectly. If direct importing can more than double his net profit, bringing it up to $1.90 per item sold, it becomes a genuine bonanza. Of course, not all direct im-

161

porting is so rewarding, but a much lower rate of profit is also acceptable, particularly if volume is high.

Table 2. United States General Imports of Principal Commodities (Value in millions of dollars).

Commodity	1963	1964	1965	1966	1967	1968	1969
Glassware	27	34	36	46	48	57	62
Pottery	63	69	75	82	85	106	133
Clothing	395	451	543	608	649	855	1106
Footwear	124	140	160	190	263	388	488
Travel goods, handbags and small leather goods	28	40	50	56	72	95	97
Toys and games	68	85	90	107	126	171	207
Sporting goods	55	56	66	73	86	112	141
Jewelry and related articles	36	34	33	41	44	55	66
Electric household appliances, radios, etc.	244	291	296	343	341	375	430

Source: U.S. Department of Commerce, *Overseas Business Reports, March 1970*, pp. 12, 13, 15.

The relative importance of many of the functions of the import buyer will differ from those of the buyer of domestic products. For example, the import buyer will have to give special consideration to transportation expenses. Because ocean freight rates are based primarily on bulk rather than on weight, the buyer must use cost per cubic foot as his yardstick. This forces his attention on compactness of an item and packaging. Profits may hinge on how well an item can be nested, or perhaps reinforced to avoid the necessity of bulky supporting packing materials.

The domestic buyer will usually protect himself by testing the salability of an item before making an important commitment. However, the long interval required to bring a foreign-made item to market will usually force the import buyer to obligate himself without the added safeguard of testing. Also, if the foreign-made item is not completely manufactured in one factory, the various component parts must be timed to arrive for assembly so that the finished product reaches the point of export on schedule.

The import buyer will spend much more of his time traveling than does the buyer of domestic goods, who most often is called on

162

in his office by vendors. Moreover, language differences will compel the import buyer to rely on agents who speak both languages, and direct communication with sources of supply will often be impossible.

The import buyer will also have to concern himself with different forms and procedures. Letters of credit are the chief method of financing imports into the United States.[2] They are clear and irrevocable commitments by the importing company and provide for the allocation of dollars, which may be necessary several months before the goods are actually received. Domestic and foreign banks skilled and experienced in all phases of importing will be helpful in preventing problems and in handling the mechanics of importing, but the buyer needs to know, for example, that the letter of credit must include an accurate description of the goods, the bill of lading and all necessary licenses. He must be certain that the marine insurance describes the coverage exactly. He must be well aware of his responsibilities with regard to the genuineness of documents, the solvency of the companies or individuals involved, as well as the quality and quantity of the goods themselves.

But despite the risks and increased responsibilities, the continued growth of interest on the part of mass merchandisers in direct importing shows that potential profits far outweigh the added costs and buying problems. The individual buyer will find the different world of import buying challenging and exciting, but he must be well informed on the problems he will encounter so that he will be able to solve them more effectively.

COPYING AN EXISTING ITEM AT A LOWER PRICE

A Christmas selling period has just ended in which an American-made toy has had a great first-season success. Judging from the eagerness of children and parents, it is almost certain that the

---

[2]A letter of credit is a letter addressed by a banker to a person to whom credit is given, authorizing that person to draw on the maker of the note up to a certain sum; the importing company places these sums with the banker who then advances them to the foreign agent or manufacturer.

popularity of this new toy will carry over one more year and probably longer. The retail price set by the toy's one and only manufacturer was high. Since the demand for the item was greater than the supply he was encouraged to concentrate on production rather than on cost reduction and control.

The experienced buyer knows that the toy can be copied in the Orient and imported to sell profitably at one-half its present price. He is also aware that toy importers and competing buyers are considering various ways to merchandise the item. What action should he take?

We are assuming that the buyer's company is one of the larger mass merchandisers with a record for being quick to capitalize on foreign buying opportunities and the organization to do so. In this instance, the opportunity to copy this item and profit from direct importing looks good. A continuing demand seems assured for a long enough period in which to bring the item to market. The market itself is big enough to warrant investment and management's attention. And since the first-year retail price of the item was high, there is plenty of margin between total costs and the planned selling price.

Obviously, the opportunity for extra profit will be the dominating factor in deciding whether or not to import this toy directly. But two other factors are important. A company that has painstakingly and at great expense set up an import division staffed with capable specialists must take advantage of such favorable opportunities to build the volume necessary to support such an operation. Also, if other firms are planning to exploit the same item, it is necessary to take aggressive defensive action to maintain a strong competitive position.

Assuming that the buyer and his merchandising superiors do decide to import the item directly, their course of action will depend largely on the degree of integration of the import division. The most complete divisions will not only have their own foreign representatives, but will have offices and even factories abroad as well. Smaller import divisions may have none of these assets; instead they will deal directly with manufacturers through foreign agents in those markets or by sending their buyer to the exporting country. If a foreign manufacturer is big enough to have offices and showrooms in this country, it is even possible for a buyer to import directly without ever leaving the country.

Copying Fashion Items

The consumer of a fashion item is usually less interested in its intrinsic value and the cost of its ingredients than in its fashion-rightness—a vague, elusive quality. The profit margins of a fashion item may therefore be greater than those for imported toys whereas its salability may be less sure and its popularity more fleeting. Size and color become added considerations not usually associated with toys. Not only must sizes and colors be accurate, but they must also be in the right proportions to meet the demand. A store's sales of a fashion-right, well-priced import come to a grinding halt if the most popular sizes and colors are sold out first; and the net profit is dissipated in markdowns of remainders.

Since fashion items grow obsolete rather quickly, it is essential that they be brought to the point of sale with the utmost speed. A retailer's import organization must learn to be quick to evaluate a fashion opportunity and quicker to execute it. Some mass merchandisers have advanced to the point where they or their representatives attend such style events as Paris openings. Great competence is required for a retailer's buying staff to make high-risk fashion commitments in a foreign market, but accurate forecasting will be extremely profitable and copies of Parisian styles will lend prestige that the mass merchandiser may feel is important to establish with his customers as well as with his store personnel. Of course, fashion advisers who become over-enthusiastic about far-out styles or who misread the preferences of a store's clientele can cause serious losses.

Before a buyer advises his merchandising superiors to copy and import a new fashion item that has already achieved considerable success—for example, a boot or a casual type of shoe for ladies—he will undoubtedly have the answers to the following questions:

Is the market big enough to warrant the necessary time and investment to bring the item to the point of sale?

Is it "his" market? Are the retailer's stores the right type to exploit this opportunity? Will the item enhance the store's reputation? Is it perhaps too chic for the store's customers?

Is the demand likely to be strong and sustained enough to allow time for design, manufacture, delivery, and merchandising of the item?

Can the item be reasonably duplicated at a price that will attract customers and still yield a good profit?

How quickly can delivery be accomplished? Can manufacture keep up if a strong demand develops?

When all these matters have been resolved to his satisfaction and the item is imported, the mass-merchandise retailer will not only have made a profit, but will also have brought fashion merchandise to his type of customer at prices within their means. The result will be the perfect combination of a happy retailer and happy customers.

Importing Other Lines

Toys and fashion are short-lived, speculative lines, but much more import volume is accounted for by lines with a long-term, year-round sales appeal. Some playthings like inflatable toys, stuffed animals, wheel toys, and balls are likely to have a sustained market for several years. Wearing apparel less subject to fashion trends, such as boys' clothing and hosiery of many kinds, is a relatively stable import category.

Other important classifications of import merchandise include chinaware, electronic items of many kinds, jewelry, leather and rubber goods, footwear, gloves, curtains, glassware, Christmas decorations, sporting goods, yarns, and piece goods. Here the importing retailer is relieved of the absolute necessity of obtaining delivery for a specific date. A few weeks' difference in the arrival date of a new pattern of dinnerware, or of a hair dryer with a new attachment, or of a lighter-weight man's work shoe, will not bring the grey hairs that are caused by the delivery of a summer fashion item on August first.

But even these less volatile merchandise categories have consumer demand characteristics calling for precise timing and planning. Perhaps the new item is scheduled to meet anticipated competitive action; or possibly the old replaced item is being phased out on a schedule which makes space for the new item at a specific time. And even the most staple basic goods must fit into a retailer's overall merchandise plan and investment scheme. Stores must have a steady flow of attractive, promotable merchandise for a smooth operation. Concentrated deliveries of large quantities of many lines cause display, storage, and investment problems. On the other hand, periods without the excitement of fresh stocks depress sales.

Cheaper foreign labor is the decisive factor in the importing of many items, especially when devising means of producing a comparatively expensive item at a lower price for mass marketing. But copied items are only a part of the importing story. The products, arts, and crafts of numerous foreign countries are in great demand in American stores because they are distinctive and have qualities not found in domestic items in the same category. Such products include German cutlery, English woolens, giftware and novelties from many lands, woodenware, earthenware, wickerware, and glassware.

Certain countries specialize in particular categories because of centuries-old skills unknown to the workers of other countries, or because of design qualities that are different and unique, or because of an abundance of basic materials such as special woods and metals. Specialized products that are important enough to be a vital part of a country's economy are likely to be carefully supported and nurtured by its government. Its officials and industrialists are usually eager to present their products conveniently and attractively to foreign buyers.

The distinctive qualities of foreign-made items are often so attractive that they are copied by American manufacturers rather than the reverse. This copying is usually made possible and profitable by applying the techniques of mass production to items made abroad by hand or by other less efficient methods.

167

WEIGHING THE RISKS OF DIRECT IMPORTING

If the demand for foreign-made products is so great, and the profits to be gained from the direct importing of these products are so attractive, why don't all mass merchandisers hasten to do so? Why do they continue to use the services of middlemen-importers? There are several reasons:

Staff Requirements. The building and maintenance of a skilled and effective import division are expensive and demand big, continuous volume to be profitable. An occasional importing success is not enough to support such an operation. Import buying also requires close, time-consuming attention from a top company officer if effective planning and control are to be maintained. And if this executive is unable to recruit and develop skilled importing personnel, he will be compelled to travel extensively himself at considerable cost to his time.

Investment. Not only does importing entail the extra costs of ocean freight, tariffs, customs duties, and insurance, but it also necessitates the advancement of funds far beyond what is required for domestic purchases. Payments for imports must be made when the merchandise is shipped from a foreign port, whereas domestic merchandise is not usually paid for until 10 to 30 days after it has been received by the store. The effect of importing on investment dollars is therefore considerable. Planned turnover is also reduced by this extended commitment.

Operating Risks. Domestic purchasing does not involve such risks as unsettled international conditions, inflation and deflation of currencies, variations in tariff costs and in the interpretation of tariff classes, varying customs costs, water damage, breakage, and pier theft. If the buyer is dealing with unstable factories, agents, or shippers, there is always the risk of financial instability and unreliability, and the possibility of bankruptcy before the completion of the transaction.

Buying and Product Risks. Because import commitments are

longer range and are usually in larger quantities than domestic purchases, all the risks that occur with the passage of time are intensified. Product obsolescence may take place faster than was anticipated when the item was on the drawing board. A newer, better product may cut into the market acceptance of the item. Fashions may change. The foreign manufacturer may make a small mistake which cheapens or impairs the attractiveness of the item, yet restitution may be impossible or unenforceable. Buying mistakes become more expensive. The retailer buying indirectly through importer-middlemen minimizes these risks. The retailer who imports directly is bound by longer and larger commitments and lives daily with all of them.

However, there are several ways by which the mass merchandiser and his buying staff can gain many of the great benefits of direct importing without incurring all the risks. For example, it is regular practice for many retailers without highly skilled, fully staffed import divisions to import in a very limited way. Dealings with importer-middlemen may lead to an association with foreign agents who present an opportunity to bypass the middleman and his function in one category. A mass merchandiser may have an especially competent buying division in a particular merchandise classification which naturally expands into direct importing. Another company may have an executive with a flair for the importing of certain lines. Some industries may have more competent and reliable foreign agents who make direct importing of their special categories less risky. (Conversely, importer-middlemen of some lines of merchandise may be so skilled that the rewards of direct importing may not be as great by comparison.) Certain foreign governments are more receptive to buying organizations from other countries and are, therefore, more desirable sources; direct importing may be limited to these more cooperative areas.

Thus retailers and their buying divisions may penetrate the world of direct importing in varying degrees. Some plunge heavily into import buying and then withdraw, at least partly, when experience proves less rewarding than hoped. Others continue to expand their direct importing operations with a consistent record of successful profit-making.

11

The Role of the Buyer in Private Brand Development

Several reasons underlie Sears, Roebuck's policy of promoting its own brands. Selling other brands does not, for instance, help build Sears' own reputation; further, the company has refused to risk dependence upon an "outside" branded source, from which it might conceivably be cut off at any time. Sears further feels that its own quality is at least as reliable as that of the most widely advertised other brands and that the tremendous amount of advertising it puts behind its own brands is equal to, or greater than, that of most other national advertisers. Also, since the company unconditionally guarantees its own goods, it feels that it must have its own standards of quality and be able at all times to control that quality. Finally, of course, there is the fact that Sears' whole merchandising operation is posited primarily upon the goods it procures . . . and it has invested too much money in merchandise development to fail to capitalize upon it through the exploitation of its own brands.[1]

Private brands are those products whose design and price are controlled by the retailer and which carry the identifying name of the retailer or a special name of his choice. As E. B. Weiss has pointed out, we have three basic types of brands. These are:

1. The manufacturer's *advertised* brand.
2. The distributor's controlled *and* advertised brand (the

[1]Emmet and Jeuck, *op. cit.,* p. 420.

170

"distributor" may be a giant retailer, a wholesaler, or a voluntary or cooperative group.)

3. The *true* private brand—which is a brand with no advertising, with little or no consumer recognition or standing, and which may be sponsored by a manufacturer, by a wholesaler, or by a retailer.[2]

Retailers typically start out with the "true" private brand. Then, if successful, they gradually move into advertising their private brands as they work on the development of the reputation of the total store. Sears, Roebuck, Montgomery Ward, and J. C. Penney are the outstandingly successful examples in this area. Of course, the bigger the retailer the greater the opportunity for private branding because larger quantities can be produced more economically and the overhead expenses can be spread over greater volume. The growing concentration of retailing in fewer hands presages more and more private branding.

THE CASE FOR THE PRIVATE BRAND

In 1960, ten large chains did an average of 15 percent of their volume in private brands. In 1965 the figure was 24 percent. By 1970 it had jumped to 32.8 percent of volume and further development is planned. There are obviously many important advantages to be gained from a private brand program.

Profit Margins

The retailer of private brands can set and control his own profit margins. Of course, his pricing is limited by what the consumer will pay for in volume but he is not at the mercy of the nationally established brand manufacturer who may choose to set his margin allowances below standards acceptable to the retailer. Moreover, the competition of a strong private brand may force the advertised brand manufacturer to raise his profit margins.

[2]E. B. Weiss, *op. cit.*, pp. 67-68.

Private branding also frees the retailer from the dogfight of discounting established brands. Price wars on famous brands to maintain competitive popularity can wipe out net profit in whole categories of merchandise. Profit is also improved when private branding brings the factory closer to the retail level, thereby eliminating the manufacturer's advertising and selling expenses, and other middleman costs.

Control

The private brander not only controls his percentage of profit margin, but he can also determine his own price points and the breadth of his selection. If he wishes to compete in a lower price range than a national brand covers, he may do so. If he chooses to concentrate on a narrower range of items in a given category than the national brander is urging, he is free to do so.

He is in a better position to control the depth as well as the breadth of his model stocks by setting his own packing quantities and assortments by type, color, or size. He can tailor his display space, his promotional efforts, and the timing of deliveries better with his own brands. Manufacturers of strong national brands can bring heavy pressure on retailers to take on large quantities of new merchandise that is unproven and may be unsuccessful. National brand manufacturers may also require minimum shipments that are too large for proper turnover in many stores; they may have unfavorable discount terms and their deliveries may be slow. It is also possible that the national brand manufacturer will have a selected list of prestige customers who will get preference in delivery and service. The private brander is in a stronger position to resist such inconveniences and pressures, and, thereby, to control his own operation.

Customer Loyalty

The successful private brand sells the store, rather than the manufacturer, to the customer. The consumer who is sufficiently impressed with the attractiveness, quality, utility, and/or price of a private brand item to buy it again must return to the same store to

172

do so and will, for her convenience, buy other things there as well. On the other hand, the purchaser of a nationally branded item may be drawn to a retailer by low price, but little loyalty has been established and the same customer can be drawn elsewhere by an equally attractive price. The big discounters aggressively built their hard-won and well-deserved reputation for customer savings by sharply cutting prices of famous brands in widely selected categories of merchandise. But once firmly established, they saw the wisdom of building their customers' confidence in the store as a whole, as an umbrella under which the acceptance of a strong private brand program could be built. Like other innovative retailers before them, the discounters discovered the long-range advantages of building customer loyalty to the store through private branding rather than to the manufacturer through cutting prices on national brands.

THE CASE FOR THE MANUFACTURER'S ADVERTISED BRAND

The advocates of the nationally advertised brand can also present a strong case. In addition to the frequent emotional charge that private brands are "bloody parasites" riding the coattails of the manufacturers' brands, there are also a number of calmer and more reasoned arguments.

President H. B. Cunningham of the S. S. Kresge Co., operator of the highly successful K-mart discount department stores, when asked about his company's private labeling policy, summarized the case for the nationally advertised brands very well:

> The discount industry came into existence importantly when the required gross margins of conventional department stores had increased to the level where a low margin operator could profitably sell national brand merchandise at a substantial discount.
> Despite the success of leading national retailers in developing private brands, Kresge is strongly oriented to national brand merchandising. It is only in the sale of national brands where dramatic selling price advantage can be so clearly demonstrated.
> National brand merchandise offers the customer not only the

image but the fact of time-proven products. The quality of a private brand item may be equal to its national brand counterpart, but the decision to buy involves not only utility but psychological factors of assurance and pride of ownership. We think that it is a mistake to underestimate the power of national brand advertising in pre-selling merchandise for the self-service retailer. [3]

National Brands Draw Traffic

When manufacturers have spent millions to establish the desirability of their products in the minds of customers, why shouldn't retailers take advantage of this fact? Why shouldn't they promote these popular products to draw consumers into their stores and to sell them when they are there? The response to the sharp pricing or to the attractive presentation of nationally known items is certainly going to be better than to an unknown brand for which no comparison exists in the customer's mind. Also, national brands are largely pre-sold and require a minimum of selling effort and time, thus delivering better sales per square foot and lower selling wage cost.

Private Brands Lack the Flexibility of National Brands

New products, new markets, new trends, new selling and advertising angles are more likely to come from the minds and drawing boards of national branders and their highly-skilled staffs and agencies. With many more outlets as their target than any one retailer has, national brand manufacturers can afford a concentration of effort that should produce better results. Consequently, the private brander, who is restricted in distribution to his own stores, is more likely to be effective with standard, basic goods. For the more innovative, faddish, and high-style products, the private brander is apt to continue to rely on national brands to maintain his reputation for up-to-dateness.

Even in standard, basic goods the private brand retailer may have little flexibility. To obtain the lowest possible cost price, he will have contracted for as large a quantity of an item and its packaging

[3]*The Discount Merchandiser,* March 1969, p. 46.

174

ingredients as he safely can. He is less able to change his manufacturing formula to add a fresh, highly salable ingredient or to give a new twist to his packaging. By the time he has used up the quantity contracted for, he may be merchandising an obsolete, slow-selling product. Without his investment in the private brand item, he would have been free to choose among national brands at once and to have the newest developments in his stores as soon as they became available.

National Brands Trade-Up a Store's Image

Retailers struggling to create a fashion-conscious, up-to-date, innovative, and quality-minded image for their stores can do so more easily by associating themselves with prestigious manufacturers' brands than through their own brands. In an increasingly affluent society and in an economy where costs of doing business as a percentage of sales are climbing steadily, mass merchandisers have the opportunity to both improve their images and sell higher priced merchandise by promoting nationally advertised brands.

Private Brands Are More Expensive Than Is Sometimes Admitted

In addition to the obviously heavy expenses of package design, there are hidden, indirect expenses associated with private branding. In the first place, private branding requires a higher degree of buying skill. True quality comparisons must be made, usually with the help of laboratory testing. Superficial examination and quick acceptance of items are inadequate when longer-term commitments are being made to products intended to project and build the retailer's reputation for value and quality. The buyer and merchandiser must be able to judge the selling merits of their packaging in competition with established brands. Mistakes can be very costly. Quantities of an unsuccessful private brand item must be sold by reducing the prices sharply or by leaving them in the investment for a long period of time, thereby slowing turnover and using valuable display space.

Private brands not only need greater buying skill than is required for the mere selection of one national brand over another, but they also demand more attention. Even in the most basic types of merchandise like screwdrivers, writing paper, or boys' shorts, there will be competitive developments and price changes which demand re-examination of the whole item and package. Product and packaging developments occur so quickly in many volatile categories that the entire theme and design of a private brand program needs a complete overhaul within two years, and all the risks and heavy costs must be assumed again. These risks and costs must be weighed when comparing the net profitability of a private brand program with the merchandising of nationally advertised brands in the same category.

Concentration on Private Brand Development May
Leave the Door Wide Open to New Forms of Competition

Totally unknown retailers can move in and entrench themselves on the strength and prestige of nationally known brands. The big discounters used this method to establish themselves, as did the small sidestreet health and beauty aids discounters. The retailer who becomes too preoccupied with his private brand program to merchandise the nationally known brands competitively may be building opportunities for present as well as future competitors.

ITEMS MOST SUITED TO PRIVATE BRANDING

The decision to add an item to a category in which the company's name and/or its brand have already achieved some customer acceptance is a simple one compared with the decision to develop a "true" private brand that has little or no pre-acceptance. Retailing giants like Sears, Roebuck, Montgomery Ward, and J. C. Penney have reached the point where the extensive advertising of their private brands has entrenched them as strongly as national brands in many categories. The customer confidence that has been so painstakingly built up by these three chains promises immediate acceptance of their new private brand products.

The degree of sophistication of the store's customers and the prestige that its name carries will be important factors in the selection of products for private branding. The more sophisticated urban consumer who has acquired a greater confidence in her shopping skill will purchase the private brand more often. The rural shopper, who is usually less sophisticated, is more likely to rely on the reputation of a national brand. But all customers take pride in ownership of a highly respected brand in any category. Shoppers consider the impact of a purchase on relatives or friends. A well-known expensive perfume, a famous-name lipstick, a prestigious coat label reflect the image that a customer wishes to project.

An incident from my own experience as a variety store manager provides a good illustration of the value that a prestige store name adds to a product. We were carrying the identical small fashion accessory that was being offered at an adjoining department store of considerable and well-deserved reputation. As an experiment, I first priced my item at $1.00—the same as the department store. No sales. At 79¢ there were a few sales. But not until the price was reduced to 50¢ in comparison with the department store's $1.00 were customers willing to give up the added value of the more prestigious store's name. Clearly, private brands of either fashion or basic merchandise are more likely to succeed under the name of such a store.

Whether or not a particular item is suitable for private branding will depend upon the specific characteristics it possesses, as follows:

Basic, non-volatile items with universal appeal, such as writing paper, mouthwash, and facial tissue, lend themselves to private branding. *Short-lived, volatile and faddish* items like novelty toys and fashion accessories are poor private brand risks.

Obvious value, that makes the item easy to compare with other brands, is a good characteristic in a private brand. If utility dominates the buying decision for that item, a private brand would probably be well-received; for example, a private brand clothesline that offers 100 feet for the same price as a national brand's 80 feet.

Hidden, prestige value in an item—a "blind" item whose intrinsic worth is not visible, and, therefore, cannot be weighed by the purchaser when considering the selling price—should rule out its development by a private brander. Perfume, for instance, is often bought for subjective reasons which the customer herself may not even recognize or acknowledge.

Standard construction that does not create any production problems is favorable to private branding; private branding may only be a matter of label-changing with such items as shampoos, school supplies, and small hardware. *Expensive molds,* or a category that is a broad line of many separate products, or one that requires a heavy investment or a long-term commitment to interest the manufacturer, are unsuitable for private branding.

Weak national brands that have inspired no customer preference or recognition, or feeble and erratic manufacturer service, create the right climate for the development of private brands. *Strong, dominant national brands,* on the other hand, may control their markets so well that private brands would find it hard to penetrate.

Short production runs of low volume items, without raising costs appreciably, make private branding feasible. *Costly and inefficient production,* because of a restricted market and because volume production would be required for low cost, should rule out private branding.

No complications with trademark or design infringement should be present to interfere with a private brand program. *Infringement* by the private brand on a national brand whose distinctive elements may be protected by a copyright or patent renders private branding inadvisable.

Unsatisfactory profit margins from national brands, which are commonly footballed at discount prices, invite the creation of private brands. *Satisfactory terms* and profit margins from national brands should discourage the development of private brands.

THE DEVELOPMENT OF THE PRIVATE BRAND ITEM

Once the specific categories and items have been determined for private branding, the buying-merchandising team will need to involve itself deeply in the specification of ingredients, formulas, and packaging. Other important considerations will include planned volume, number of models, sizes, and colors. Guarantee, warranty, and servicing policies must also be covered. Plans for promotion and publicity will have to be made. The manufacturer will usually be helpful in many of these areas. He is most likely experienced in the development of his own national brand or other private brands, and his advice will be invaluable. He will probably also have staff personnel skilled in design and art work.

The determination of retail price is a critical consideration in private branding. Presumably, a higher margin of profit is sought by the retailer than he is at present receiving from a national brand. And the retail price of the private brand should represent an economy over the national brand, for if a customer is giving up whatever comfort, assurance, or pride she receives from the purchase of a national brand, the very least she expects is a price economy. However, the private brand item and its packaging should not just give the immediate and strong impression of economy alone. To justify its higher price, the national brand offers customers innovation in product design, utility, or other characteristics; or it provides the strength and popularity of a well-respected name. The uppermost question in the mind of the purchaser of a private brand is not its price, but rather, its quality and utility in comparison with the national brand. It may be good pricing strategy to have the item design shout "save $3.00," or "now you can have two for the price of one," or "three times as much for your money," but most customers want to be convinced that they are not sacrificing other qualities for price. Therefore, to the extent that he can influence such decisions, the buyer should try to make low price secondary or implicit and to emphasize quality.

Since one of the prime reasons for a private brand program is to build customer loyalty to a store rather than to a brand, it becomes most important that the private brand item not only be salable but

179

also perform well in use. The customer has selected it over a national brand; she has sacrificed the greater assurance she derives from the national brand for expected quality and performance for the lower price of the private brand. She will, therefore, be more skeptical of the private brand item *throughout its life performance.* If the private brand lets her down, the store's image suffers as well.

Packaging is also critical to the development of an appealing and successful private brand. Here is an example of the great care and devotion that the J. C. Penney Co. puts into the packaging of its private brands:

> Packaging development begins with extensive research in proper package dimensions and form as well as in materials available for production requirements. The packaging buyer determines materials and total package cost, and guidelines are turned over to three package engineers and the department heads. . . .
>
> Four or five package concepts are developed and submitted to the buyer and department heads for evaluation. The copywriter meets with the buyer to determine the information about item identification, sales features, and care and use instructions that are important to self-selection display of the product. After copy is approved, it is carefully screened by the legal department for conformance to government regulations and by the Merchandise Testing Center to substantiate claims of performance. . . .
>
> Numerous layouts are made [by the design group] before finding one that has strong visual appeal, both in design and color. Every new package . . . must include strong company and product identification . . . and quality connotation of the package both individually and when in mass display.[4]

Even after an ambitious and successful private brand program has been developed, it cannot be followed blindly without checkup and re-examination. Many such programs were initiated with high hopes and some success and then foundered or trailed off into embarrassing failure and unprofitability. All retailers naturally envy the merchandiser who has an outstandingly successful private brand program, and dream of accomplishing the same. But such envy can cause an irrational reverence for private labeling that can

[4]*Packaging Digest,* February 1971, pp. 12-13.

carry a retailer too far too fast into a heavy, long-term commitment that can be an expensive disappointment.

SPECIFICATION AND BASIC BUYING

It has already been noted that private branding requires a greater degree of buying skill and specialization. It is an easy matter to enter into the private labeling of a particular item or category of merchandise by using the expert services of a manufacturer who specializes in private brand development. But such a piecemeal approach is not likely to lead to a coherent company-wide program with clearly defined, attainable goals.

For this reason, established mass merchandisers with enough sales volume to justify the employment of sufficient buyers to specialize in the purchase of a restricted group of items will encourage "specification" buying. By concentrating their efforts, such buyers will become knowledgeable enough to perform far beyond the mere selection of wares; they will participate in deciding the specifications of the merchandise—its design, as well as its physical and chemical composition. In the purchase of established, pre-sold, standardized advertised items, which are offered to a buyer pretty much on a "take-it-or-leave-it" basis, there will be very little leeway of this sort. But in areas where products can be tailored to the retailer's preferences with regard to pricing, quality, and design, as in private branding, buying by specification may take place.

However, retailers like Sears, Roebuck & Co. have gone far beyond specification buying to the complete negotiation of all aspects of buying, or "basic" buying. This procedure involves the decision by a retailer, his buying-merchandising staff, and his research staff that sufficient market exists for a product in his stores; the selection of potential manufacturers by studying their capacities, capabilities, and location; the development of design and product specifications, and pricing and profit goals after an analysis of competitive products; and negotiation with and education of the supplier in the production, packaging, and transportation of the item.

181

Basic Buying Planning

Suppose that Company X, a very large mass merchandiser with strong private brands in many merchandise categories, is considering the addition of dusting powder to its line of private brand toiletries. The following planning and action might take place:

Determining Sales Potential. The annual sales potential might be set at $150,000. This estimate might be based on the 5 percent that dusting powders represent of the total cosmetic sales of other brands. This figure would then be applied to total sales of the cosmetics private brand as a rough guide to expected sales volume. Because dusting powder is a potential gift item at Mother's Day and Christmas, the possibility of promotions and extra sales at those times would be considered.

Analyzing the Competition. Competitive products in every important brand would be analyzed from all angles to identify their most desirable characteristics.

Setting Prices. Retail price point and markon goals would be set, thus establishing cost limits. Assuming that competitive products range in retail price from 69 cents to $5.00, Company X selects $1.50 as its price because this is considered the point at which the volume goal can be reached. A good value and a salable item can be produced at this price, and it places the retailer in the range in which he wants to be in relation to his competition and his company's image. Markon is set at 50 percent, which exceeds that given by the nationally advertised brand by a margin probably set by overall company policy.

Selecting Design, Ingredients, and Packaging. The basic buying of the item's design, components, and packaging then begins. The shape, color, and decoration are selected, very likely to fit into a pattern previously set for related items. If the basic design of the powder box does not already exist, the costs of a special mold must be contemplated. Having decided on the weight, strength, and size

182

of the box, the grade of the powder and its fragrance will be considered. There are wide variations in both of these qualities and each is crucial to ultimate salability and customer satisfaction. The powder puff can be constructed in many different ways and will probably have an inscription to be decided on. Packaging must also be determined. Will each item have its own attractive display box or will the item be packaged in bulk by itself in a shipping carton of 6 or 12 pieces? The package must help the sale and be in the ideal unit for stock replenishment by the average-sized store.

Establishing Standards of Quality. Quality control standards will be established both for the original production and the maintenance of quality.

Planning Merchandising Strategy. The merchandising strategy for the item will then be determined. Perhaps it will be decided to limit initial distribution to the large- and medium-sized stores, omitting the small stores at least until the item has proved itself. How the new item will be introduced, and in what quantities, will be worked out with the sales promotion and advertising staffs. There may also be instructions as to display grouping, model stock quantities, and/or displacement of another item.

Obviously, basic buying of this sort gives the retailer complete price, quality, and design control over his purchases. It makes long-range planning more feasible. But, just as obviously, it has its risks. It requires substantial item volume and it calls for rare buying skills and uncommon knowledge of production costs.

THE FUTURE OF PRIVATE BRANDING

There are certain straws in the wind indicating trouble ahead for the manufacturer's national brand in its struggle with the retailer's private brand. National brand advertisers are concerned with youth's lack of loyalty to brands compared to that of their elders. Although the young show a comparable brand awareness, their passion for individuality and, occasionally, their hostility to the establishment have been noted by advertising experts to carry over into their attitudes toward recognized brands. Manufacturers are also disturbed by reports that the growing amount of advertising and the increasing number of printed impressions to which the consumer is exposed daily tend to dilute the impact of their own particular messages.

Manufacturers are more and more aware that the retailer holds many trump cards in the development of his own brands. And not to be underestimated is the retailer's display-space power. He can put his own brand on the easy-to-reach shelf and relegate the manufacturer's brand to the "stoop-for" shelf. This is a mighty weapon in a retailer's strategy of building customer confidence in private brands and loyalty to the store as a whole.

The battle of the brands—national vs. private—will continue. Indications are strong that private branding will grow as a percentage of the typical mass merchandiser's sales volume. Nine out of ten major variety chains are planning to substantially increase the proportion of their volume that private brands produce. As mass merchandisers become even larger and better established, they will keep on trying to build customer loyalty to themselves, to instill confidence in their stores as *the* place to shop. Private brands will continue to be a very important part of this campaign.

12

The Buyer, the Law, and the Consumer Movement

Today's shopping center numbers in excess of 100 stores and attracts the "universal" shopper. This customer, influenced by consumer research and government-sponsored "consumer protection" departments, has a behavioral pattern that differs sharply from the preciseness of the past. The ability of a store to draw this pattern, to measure its own image, and to act on the results will dictate future success.[1]

There exists today a maze of confusing, contradictory, and changing legislation which affects the buyer's day-to-day activities. If not already on the law books, legislation is being urged or argued in the courts or Congress. In addition to the formidable body of Federal law and many local regulations, individual customers are taking their complaints to court with greater frequency, consumer groups are becoming more and more active, and continuing differences between retailers and their suppliers demand legal interpretation and knowledge.[2]

---

[1]Ernest Dichter, Ph.D., President and Research Director, Institute for Motivation Research, *Department Store Management,* December 1969, p. 28.

[2]This chapter does not pretend to offer a definitive discussion of the law as it affects retailing. The reader seeking more detailed information on this subject is referred to the texts listed on the following page.

Not one buyer in a thousand has any real legal training, or the time to investigate the details of the law. But the buyer who aggressively goes his merry way with crossed fingers and no compliance with or knowledge of the law is exposing himself and his company to costly risks. All mass merchandisers have expert legal talent available who can easily be consulted by the buyer. But the buyer should know enough about the law to avoid the great majority of its pitfalls and to seek expert help when he feels that he may be in possible violation. Moreover, some knowledge of the law in reference to the granting of promotional allowances will enable the buyer to take fuller advantage of the profit opportunities such allowances provide.

FEDERAL LEGISLATION

Almost from their inception in the early 1900's chain stores have had to fight restrictive and punitive legislation because of the threat, or imagined threat, they presented to the small, independent merchant. Chain store development brought lower prices, better merchandise selections, and brighter, more attractive stores. The public flocked to the chain outlets and they prospered. The independent merchant fought back vigorously and had the political muscle in his community to make his feelings felt strongly in Congress. A bitter running battle ensued that provided headline news for years. It was finally settled in the late 1930's and 1940's in the court of public opinion. Chain stores had won such a secure position in the hearts and pocketbooks of the American

---

Boris Emmet and John E. Jeuck, *Catalogues and Counters* (Chicago: University of Chicago Press, 1950), pp. 604-622.

Myron S. Heidingsfield and Albert B. Blankenship, *Marketing* (New York: Barnes & Noble, 1967), Chapter 9.

Godfrey M. Lebhar, *Chain Stores in America: 1859-1962* (New York: Chain Store Publishing Corporation, 1963), pp. 107-390.

Manual of Federal Trade Regulations Affecting Retailers, National Retail Merchants Association.

Charles F. Phillips and Delbert J. Duncan, *Marketing,* 5th ed. (Chicago: Irwin, 1964), pp. 784-793.

public that, through the highly-organized efforts of the chains and their committees in Washington, they were able to fight off crippling legislation. But it was a close battle at times and it brought into being greater inter-chain cooperation, as well as a better understanding of the chains' community position and responsibilities.[3]

The Sherman Antitrust Act of 1890 was the first legislation to prohibit agreements that would restrict free trade by price fixing or by refusals to sell to certain customers. The Clayton Act of 1914 strengthened the Sherman Act by forbidding price agreements and promotions that would probably lessen competition. The Robinson-Patman Act of 1936 put more teeth into the Sherman and Clayton Acts and is of special interest to retailers. It outlawed price discrimination by vendors, and thereby prevented large retailers from using their size to secure price advantage. In its enforcement of Robinson-Patman, however, the Government has increasingly pointed to the retailer, rather than the vendor, as the violator and the one to check on. The Federal Trade Commission is charged with the responsibility of enforcing this legislation and it has consistently taken the position that buyers must not use the size of their companies to "induce" special (and therefore unfair) prices or other differentials.

Other Federal laws that affect specific retailers and buyers are the Flammable Fabrics Act, the Wool Products Labeling Act, the Textile Fiber Products Indentification Act, and the Fur Products Labeling Act. And there is almost always pending legislation of concern to retailers in general.

Truth in Packaging

Federal regulations which require that the net weights and measures of items be clearly shown have been on the books for many years. A list of ingredients must appear on the label of drugs, cosmetics, foods, and some fabrics. In 1966 the Fair Packaging and Labeling Act became law. Based on knowledge gained from past

---

[3]For a comprehensive account of these events, see Godfrey M. Lebhar, *Chain Stores in America, op. cit.*

enforcement experience, it spelled out and defined the law in such a way that it put more teeth into Federal authority over industry. But the emphasis of the Act is on voluntary arrangements through industry-government cooperation in working out packaging and labeling standards. Every retailer should be most interested in working with manufacturers and the Government toward practical solutions to packaging and labeling problems. Such cooperation will not only protect the consumer, but it will also prevent dissatisfaction which would react negatively on the store's reputation, and eventually on its net results.

When examining an item presented by a manufacturer, the buyer should be sure to study the printed message on the package because of its marketing importance. In weighing the value of the item in relation to its cost, the buyer must recognize the ingredients and understand how they contribute to the use of the item as stated on the package. It is a simple matter for him to learn the law that refers to correct labeling and proper descriptions for his categories of merchandise. When details appear to be missing or exaggerated, or if he is inexperienced in any area, his most reliable suppliers will be able to inform him, or he may consult his company's legal counsel. And he must keep abreast of changing regulations. As of August 1969, the Fair Packaging and Labeling Act passed by Congress three years earlier was still being interpreted and the courts were still in doubt as to its exact intent. Further definition of the meaning and small print of such legislation will always require the continuing attention of buyers and merchandisers.

In areas such as housewares appliances, it is natural for the customer to want to know how much service she can expect from an item and what recourses to take if it does not perform as expected. The manufacturer and retailer, therefore, will both be interested in supplying this information as positively as possible to help sell the merchandise. But they will also wish to guarantee or warrant serviceability in words that do not leave them open to unjustified claims for refund or replacement or repair. The Federal Government's watchdog in this area, the Federal Trade Commission, offers some definite recommendations. It urges that the general tendency of the guarantee be a genuine attempt to protect the consumer rather than the manufacturer. It prescribes that the manufacturer and buyer check for the following: Is the guarantor named? Does the guarantee say what products or parts are covered? Does it give the length of the guarantee period? Does it tell the customer what he must do to secure redress? Do all statements on the guarantee match? Is it set in a type size that is easy to read? Here again, legal counsel should be sought when compliance is in doubt.

The Pricing of Merchandise

Fair Trade laws allow manufacturers to set minimum resale prices for their goods and require their wholesale and retail outlets to conform. Once enforced in 45 states, Fair Trade has been eroded by other legislation and by court attack and is now enforced in only a few of these states; manufacturers are generally not eager to enforce it at all. Manufacturers sought through Fair Trade to please their many small customers by protecting them against so-called "cut-throat" competition by large retailers and discounters. Some manufacturers of prestige items felt that promotion of the sale of their products chiefly by cut-price appeal tarnished the image of those items. They believed that their products would prosper more if stores promoted through superior display and salesmanship rather than through lowered prices.

These arguments in favor of Fair Trade have yielded for the most part to the opposition to this form of price maintenance. Manufacturers took careful note of the huge sales volume they were not getting from the price-cutters. They became less and less eager to protect their own retail prices when they saw what a stimulant lowered prices were to the sales of their competitors' brands. Manufacturers striving to maintain retail prices often lost as customers the largest-scale retailers, who felt that vendors should not tell them how to run their businesses. Mass merchandisers and their buying divisions usually oppose resale price maintenance because the freedom to use pricing as a merchandising and promotional tool is very important to them. Also, their efficiency as retailers makes it possible for them to price below others and still obtain a proper return on investment.

189

Price Advertising

The buyer must describe his merchandise in the best possible light to sell it, but at the same time he must avoid deceiving the public with untruths, half-truths, and corner-cutting. It is his responsibility to guide his advertising and promotional staff in the legal use of price-savings and price-comparison figures and wordings. Not only is the law clear on the subject of misrepresentation, but once customers have been deceived, they are likely to remember who deceived them; and deception in just one merchandise category, even if unintentional, can reflect seriously on the good name of a vast organization.

The courts will hold that large-scale retailers should know enough about what they buy and sell to spot misrepresentation by their suppliers. Once he is sure that the supplier has represented his merchandise properly, the buyer must in turn represent it properly to his buying committee, staff organization, and stores. He should know more about the details of items in his categories than does anyone else in his company, and his management should be able to rely on him to use his knowledge to avoid both customer deception and all litigation.

The Federal Trade Commission has made it clear that it frowns on and may prosecute the following practices:

Advertising of prices as lower than those of competitors ("comparable value," "retail value") when such claims cannot be supported within the same trading area.

Prices advertised as "reduced," "formerly," "regularly," or "sale" when the item or items have not actually been offered for a reasonable period of time at the higher price.

Claims of "free," "two for the price of one," and "1 cent sales" must be without gimmicks or substitution of items.

Sub-standard merchandise ("seconds," "irregulars," and "damaged goods") must be clearly identified as such in all promotion.

The Commission has also stated that the retailer is responsible for the "net impression" of his advertising: in other words, the

190

consumer may be considered misled by the omission as well as by the misstatement of facts, if the total impact of the ad is one of deception. Limitations of products as to strength, side-effects, aging, and dangers from improper use must be clearly and conspicuously stated on labels and in advertising.

The prevalence of aggressive price and comparison advertising will vary greatly among types of retailers and classes of merchandise. But most mass merchandisers rely strongly on such basic promotional appeals to draw traffic, and they will also depend on their buyers to know the applicable legal regulations.

Cooperative Advertising

Non-retailers and the public may not be aware that many of the store advertisements they see in newspapers and other media are paid for either in part or wholly by suppliers seeking greater cooperation for their products from stores at the point of sale. These payments and the resultant ads are valued as most important merchandising tools by the manufacturer and are also a great help to the retailer's advertising budget.

The importance of cooperative advertising to the entire distribution process may be appreciated by the estimate that it comes to about $500 million annually, and that about 30 percent of the total advertising costs of department stores are supported by cooperative advertising allowances.

This large dollar amount attracted the curiosity of lawmakers as far back as the 1930's. Since preferential payments could easily be made to the disadvantage of the small retailer whom Congress sought to protect, cooperative advertising has continued to be the object of legislation, Supreme Court decisions, and Federal Trade Commission rulings. Fortunately for the retailer and buyer, most of the burden of compliance rests on the manufacturer. But the Commission considers the retailer responsible if he accepts more than his proportionate share of monies for cooperative advertising or other services.

Discrimination in the giving or receiving of advertising and promotional allowances has long been forbidden by law. All forms

191

of allowances must be made available to competing retailers on "proportionately equal terms." The largest retailers may receive the largest allowances but the monies must have a corresponding relationship to the value of the services performed. The courts have also held that large retailers have a greater responsibility than small retailers to be aware of discrimination; that a buyer who feels he is getting an unusual deal should check its legality; and that any deal which the buyer himself has proposed and put through with the manufacturer is more his legal responsibility than if the manufacturer had proposed it.

The Fred Meyer Case and Its Implications. In 1963 the Government took action against Fred Meyer, Inc., a chain of food outlets on the Pacific Coast, charging discrimination in the handling of cooperative advertising allowances. The case went to the Supreme Court, whose decision was then subject to interpretation and the issuance of guidelines by the Federal Trade Commission. Substantially, these guidelines held that a supplier of promotional allowances is as responsible for giving these monies to the indirect customers of wholesalers as he is to his direct customers. In other words, the smallest independent retailer, buying entirely through a wholesaler and having no direct dealings with the manufacturer, must be treated in the same way as a mass merchandiser. While admitting that these payments should be based on the volume of purchases by a retailer, the ruling requires that *all* retailers be explicitly informed of the details of the offer to earn the monies. Affected are all forms of merchandising assistance such as advertising, prizes, catalogues, display helps, contests, and demonstrations. The manufacturer's plan must be "fair to all customers." Its availability must be known to all customers. If the basic plan is not usable by all customers, an alternative plan must be made available that is. The plan must be clearly understood and the supplier must see to it that payments under the plan are equitable.

To a certain extent, this ruling is a victory for the small retailer, who had, in effect, been excluded from these cooperative advertising funds by lack of direct contact with the producer as well as by his own failure to keep himself informed. However, the increased amount of paperwork that resulted from the Fred Meyer decision, and the greater responsibility for policing the performances of retailers to earn the allowances, have caused many vendors to give up cooperative promotion entirely. At present, manufacturers and wholesalers are finding it a big and expensive job to make these promotional allowances effective at the level, for example, of the independent drug store. The costs of administering, convincing, and implementing promotions for such small retailers are very high. Yet if these thousands of small dealers can somehow be harnessed into an effective united national campaign, they can greatly improve the total results that the manufacturer derives from his cooperative promotional funds. Some vendors, therefore, are expending their efforts to organize the promotional activities of small retailers through their wholesalers and their existing voluntary associations. Mass merchandisers and their buyers should follow such developments carefully to be sure that cooperative advertising monies are secured and used to the maximum advantage.

Exclusive Arrangements with Vendors

It is commonly accepted practice for a manufacturer to limit the number of outlets for his wares. For various reasons, exclusivity in distribution may be desirable for him, and when this is the case, the retail buyer will be active in negotiating for the exclusive arrangements. But Federal law does not allow the retailer to enter into such deals if they are judged to be part of a conspiracy with other retailers or vendors to restrain trade or to monopolize business.

As of this writing, the Rike-Kumler Company, a large Dayton, Ohio, department store, is deeply involved in a suit in which it is charged with conspiring to keep "highly desirable" lines away from smaller, local competitors. This suit may wind up in the Supreme Court as a landmark case like that of Fred Meyer, Inc. It will probably establish precedents that will greatly affect the future granting and accepting of exclusive arrangements between supplier and retailer. All retailers and manufacturers will watch the progress of this suit with great interest.

THE BUYER AND THE CONSUMER MOVEMENT

"We must recognize that across the nation the consumer is demanding to be heard. By our actions we must prove that we are listening," said James Lutz, vice president of Montgomery Ward. He went on to observe that retailers and their suppliers must respond to consumerism by "doing more, doing better, and doing it now." Products must be safer, more durable, and workable. Warranties and guarantees must make sense. Replacement parts must be available. [4]

The consumer, by buying or refusing to buy, has always been the final judge of the decisions of manufacturers and retailers. This purchasing power has inspired manufacturers and retailers to take great pains to satisfy consumers, and has brought about industry self-policing in an attempt to win consumer approval. The manufacturer does his utmost to produce articles a little more appealing in some way than those of his competitors. The retailer works to attract customers through lower prices, conveniences, and services that create more traffic and sales. The advent of mass merchandising brought pressure on manufacturers for lower prices through demonstrated marketing economies. Combined with the savings that large-scale retailing brought to distribution and selling costs, these developments benefited the buying public with lower prices and greater shopping satisfaction.

But it is becoming increasingly evident that it is not enough for industry to manufacture and sell wanted products, pay substantial taxes in support of the Government, and thereby contribute to the continuing expansion of the buying public's standard of living. Federal, state, and local governments have always had to contend with the occasional manufacturer or retailer who flagrantly violated the law. But there is a much larger gray area of consumer criticism

[4] Speaking before the Merchandising Executives Club of Chicago, as reported by *Variety Department Store Merchandiser,* December 1969, p. 2.

of manufacturers and retailers on such grounds as excessively high distribution costs, misleading if not deceptive promotion and advertising, and disregard for and lack of response to consumer interest and inquiry. These criticisms persist regardless of the fact that manufacturers and retailers, alone and in cooperation, have made great progress in all of these areas. Self-policing in matters of improved packaging, warranties, guarantees, labeling, credit terms, advertising, product safety, and product quality is increasingly effective. Consumers are better served in these areas than ever before and there is no doubt that improvement will continue on a voluntary basis. Nevertheless, the fact remains that there is a strong feeling among consumers, as reflected by their representatives in Congress, that additional protection is needed, and that the voluntary efforts of manufacturers and retailers do not sufficiently safeguard their interests.

Whether or not consumer discontent comes from the increased impersonality of retailing or from a general demand for greater social responsibility, the retailer and buyer must respond satisfactorily. Much customer discontent with retailing stems from a lack of communication and an absence of mutual understanding. The growth of self-service in mass merchandising has diminished personal contact almost to the vanishing point. Small frustrations develop that remain unresolved and grow into a feeling that the retailer is disinterested in the customer's personal buying problems. The J. C. Penney Company has thought enough about the gravity of this discontent to announce that it has established a "public affairs department" that "acknowledges our responsibility to participate in matters which may not directly affect our business, but affect the climate in which we do business."[5]

Though he usually works out of a remote office far from local community problems and away from the customers of the stores he serves, the buyer can do a great deal to help. He can make sure that the promotional and advertising materials used for his merchandise categories are always truthful and do not mislead; that labeling and

[5]As quoted in an editorial, "A Consumer Revolution," *The Discount Merchandiser,* October 1969, p. 67.

tagging do not conceal elements that will eventually disappoint the customer. The buyer can make a special point of informing customers and anticipating their questions by taking greater pains with the details of sign-writing, labeling, and so on. He can make more vigorous efforts to inform sales personnel of the limitations as well as of the selling points of products. He can tailor his assortments to fit special regional or ethnic wants. And, through store visits and communication with store personnel, he can improve his sensitivity to both the positive and negative reactions of customers to his selections and be in a better position to fulfill his role in the complete and continuing satisfaction of the consumer.

"The new consumer is not 'taking it' any longer. Probably at no time has consumer dissatisfaction and anger been so dangerous to markets. . . . Almost every company has a vast number of disgruntled, dissatisfied, and frustrated ex-lovers . . . with tremendous power. They can counteract millions of dollars of advertising by negative word-of-mouth."[6] Every member of the retailing community must face the disaffected customers. The buyer, in his central role as the selector of merchandise, and, therefore, as the one who determines its quality, must assume the responsibility for supplying his stores with salable products that will perform as expected and satisfy in use.

[6]Dr. Ernest Dichter, as quoted in "Growing Danger: The Aggrieved Customer," *Department Store Management*, December 1969, p. 28.

13

Buying as a Career

In retailing you enjoy such a constantly changing world that experience is heightened. There's no set pattern to your days. You always have to pay close attention to today as well as tomorrow and examine the possibilities in order to be able to come up with new approaches. There's a very definite excitement in this. And, unlike many other things, you are constantly confronted with the fruits of your labor in very concrete terms.[1]

Leonard Feinstein, senior vice president of Arlan's, offered the above evaluation when asked whether there was anything especially gratifying about his work that could be used to attract younger talent into the business. His statement aptly describes the buying aspect of retailing as well.

The new buyer immediately becomes a decision-maker on a small scale. He is in the enviable position of seeing the results of his efforts—"the fruits of his labors," as Mr. Feinstein calls it—on a day-to-day basis. Even in the largest retailing organization, the buyer is not a submerged cog in a vast machine. He has distinct identity and is responsible for a particular category of merchandise whose movement and results are clearly measurable.

For those who enjoy associating and working with others, buying

[1]In an interview with *The Discount Merchandiser*, November 1968, p. 111.

197

offers continuous contact with people—vendors, fellow employees, and customers. Such contacts lend an unusual variety to buying and provide an opportunity for some small emotional satisfactions which are often not available in the more routine occupations.

However, all levels and phases of retailing are very competitive and buying is no exception. Compensation in the beginning is not large, though it matches most other industries competing for manpower. Because central buying offices must adjust their schedules according to the peak demands of the stores they serve, buying is seldom a nine-to-five job. Store operations, from which the majority of buyers come, have working hours suited to customer shopping habits, which very frequently means weekend and night work. Obviously, buying is for those who will derive more than enough satisfaction from its attractions to offset its heavy demands.

BUYER QUALIFICATIONS

Above all, the buyer must be abundantly endowed with that quality which is requisite for all those who are to be happy and successful in retailing—namely, with enthusiasm for merchandising. 'Whoever does not enjoy merchandising in all its aspects, who does not derive a real satisfaction from playing a role in the successful execution of a sale or selling idea, who does not perceive the so-called "romance of retailing," had better seek a career elsewhere.

And since buying depends a great deal on team play—on the working together of many people for a common purpose—egocentrics and loners would be totally unsuitable for this type of work. The buyer's constant contact with vendor representatives, with store and top management, merchandise managers, staff personnel, and other buyers makes it necessary that he become a skillful communicator and that he communicate with enthusiasm.

The buyer must be a student of merchandise. He must be thoroughly versed in the comparative values of the merchandise categories he buys and be able to weigh their quality and workmanship. He should be capable of approaching his job with objectivity and an open mind, and should not be inclined to prejudge or to show favoritism. He should be able to give fair and unbiased consideration to the merits of a new item or vendor.

The buyer must be an accurate interpreter of consumer demand. He must know his customers and their wants. His own personal tastes or the desire to copy another retailer may mislead him if they do not square exactly with the demands of his own stores' clientele. And he must be ready at all times to recognize and react to changes in his customers' tastes.

The buyer should also be adept with figures. He should learn to interpret information quickly and well. Much of his action and decisions will be based on current figures and reports which require swift study and correlation. Computers supply information fast and abundantly, and the buyer should be able to take maximum advantage of their output.

Background and Experience

Most present-day mass-merchandising buyers are selected from within the store organization where they were either store managers or management trainees. They therefore represent a "known quantity"; they have already demonstrated a certain degree of competence and have shown that they possess the qualities most desirable for the job. In addition, it is usually good personnel policy to promote and select from within the company.

Even more important, the buyer trained in store operations can visualize the exact path that his purchase will take at the store level and, thereby, anticipate both the opportunities and the problems it may encounter. He can place himself in the position of the store manager in judging how well his purchases will perform—their salability, their packing adequacy, and the correctness of the quantity shipped. The orientation of the buyer with store management experience is likely to be toward the customer's needs, preferences, and motivations rather than the manufacturer's. Too, a "store manager quarterbacks a profit center with the same crosscurrents of decision-making (if in miniature) as one of the com-

199

pany's top brass. . . . A man comes out of the stores, not a narrow specialist, but a broad generalist." [2]

But the selection of buyers solely from the ranks of store management can lead to serious disadvantages. It carries the risks of in-breeding, of creating an unhealthy static condition in a rapidly changing industry. Years of training in the same procedures and by the same formulas may lead to a "this-is-the-way-we-have-always-done-it-this-is-the-way-we-do-it-now" attitude. Men with long experience in store management often undertake buying assignments in middle age. The advantages of maturity may be at least partly offset by a rigidity, by a lack of understanding of the young market and of the latest retailing trends. Buying should not be a late-career job for someone seeking work that requires less physical exertion. Innovation and change are not likely to come from such people.

Young companies that are trying to consolidate their early growth may not need to be invigorated by fresh ideas from outsiders, but the more mature firm benefits from the cross-fertilization of ideas that is made possible by recruiting employees with varied backgrounds. The retailer who is merchandising a new category or developing a higher fashion approach for the first time will surely need to find buyers and merchandisers with experience in these new areas. Almost certainly, the existing buying staff will lack the know-how that would enable it to launch a new, highly competitive venture.

A buyer who comes from employment with vendors will have a specialized knowledge of a particular category of merchandise that no store management experience could provide. He will be well acquainted with manufacturing processes, cost elements, and product availability. Such detailed information is very valuable to the buying process. What he lacks in store management experience and know-how may be provided by his divisional merchandise manager and by a good training program.

Successful buyers come from a wide variety of educational backgrounds. Knowing that higher education will usually produce

[2] Ben Gordon, editorial director, *Chain Store Age,* September 1969, p. 37.

a well-rounded, broad-gauged individual, chain store personnel departments seek to recruit a good percentage of college graduates—whether they be from liberal arts or business colleges, two or four year colleges, or graduate schools—for their executive training programs. Distributive Education courses at the high school level have also been very productive of better trained personnel at all retailing levels.

But the retailing industry, including buying, is full of highly successful men and women without special educational advantages—high school and grammar school graduates, or even dropouts from these levels. According to *Department Store Management* magazine: "Another indication of the degree to which things have changed in the retail establishment is the readiness with which some executives of department stores will point to the top management of many of the successful discount store chains and mass merchandisers as examples of the type of men needed to achieve success in today's marketplace. . . . 'The minority of them are college grads,' one store president noted, 'let alone Masters of Business Administration. They are simply merchants, and good ones because they concentrate solely on the fundamental principles of retailing. And they talk sense to a huge segment of the buying public.' " [3]

The ideal buying division of a mass-merchandising company should consist of a combination of buyers and merchandise managers with store and production experience. A balance should be struck between the best of the experience on which the company's success has been built and new ideas and fresh approaches to merchandising. Management should seek buyers from any and all backgrounds that can produce merchants with the desire and capabilities to do the job.

THE BUYER'S DAY

The typical buyer works with manufacturers and trades for the

[3] Interview with Charles M. Edwards, Jr., Dean of NYU's Institute of Retail Management, *Department Store Management*, May 1, 1969, p. 41.

most salable selection of merchandise at the most favorable prices and terms. He schedules timely deliveries in quantities calculated to yield maximum sales with maximum turnover. He guides stores as far as possible in the display and promotion of the merchandise, and he assists in its replenishment.

But whereas some buyers perform all of these functions, others may be required by management to concentrate heavily on only one aspect of the job. The rapid changes in all phases of retailing have had—and will continue to have—their direct and indirect impact on the buyer's role. Growth, mergers, and radical innovations, such as those growing out of the increased and imaginative use of computers, have already modified the buying function.

To better understand the buying process and the buyer's role in mass merchandising, it will be helpful to examine a typical set of problems and activities with which the buyer copes daily. The variations will be great among companies with dissimilar buying policies, among merchandise categories that require different emphases, and among firms whose varying sizes demand a greater or lesser degree of specialization of duties. But the typical buyer will be involved in each of the following activities:

The Interviewing of Vendors and Their Representatives. These interviews will usually be scheduled for certain hours and days, which will protect the buyer from frequent interruptions, and, at the same time, be considerate of the vendor's time as well. Customarily, selected morning hours of certain days are set aside for interviewing, and special appointments are made, usually in the afternoons, for the longer and more important meetings. Special consideration is often given out-of-town vendors and adjustments are made to accommodate them.

The Making of Buying Decisions. Buying decisions may be made at the interview but are more likely to be reached at a later time. Before a final decision is made and an order written, the buyer will probably wish to make comparisons with other items, review his present selection in that particular merchandise category, refer his tentative decision to his merchandise supervisors, settle on pricing, number of stores to which to distribute, and quantities to be sent to each store. He will also consider the routing and timing of deliveries, what display and promotion he will recommend, and how stocks will be replenished by the stores.

The Planning and Buying of Periodic All-Store Promotions. Such planning and buying will usually be done in advance of a sales promotion meeting involving all departments, but the buyer will always be on the alert to discover or develop suitable items for promotion. In addition to the regular buying decisions referred to above, he will need to suggest advertising placement and copy, and to plan his markon for promotions in the right mix in relation to his regular buying in order to meet his overall profit goals.

Line Reviews. Line reviews for both regular and seasonal groups of merchandise are time-consuming but valuable. These reviews are simply the assembly of all available statistical information on the sale by item of a merchandise group and the laying out of samples of these items for comparison with possible replacements. The performance of the full line is studied and its extension or contraction considered. A schedule of line reviews, with definite dates for completion of each, should be set up and followed. Line reviews pay off in many unpredictable ways by focusing attention on a group of related items from the customer's point of view. Basic items should be reviewed twice a year in this way and seasonal lines analyzed when the buying is done for that particular event.

The Daily Review of Sales and Reorder Reports. This review provides bits of information and clues that serve as the basis for quick judgments and action. Every mail and every contact, whether in person or by phone, brings some small piece of information that has value for the buyer. The buyer must always be alert to keep his fund of merchandise data current and accurate, and all opportunities to obtain this sort of feedback should receive high priority in his allotment of time.

Working the Market. Visits to the vendors' showrooms, factories, and trade shows will naturally absorb more of the time of the buyer whose office is remote from the manufacturers' headquarters, and who, therefore, may not have ready access to the lines he must see. Indeed, there are definite advantages to viewing a full line where it is most effectively displayed, especially if it is bulky and difficult to transport. Such visits also give the buyer an opportunity to see wanted items which the vendor may not have thought of presenting at the buying office. Valuable contacts with manufacturer executives other than the regular representatives are more easily made at the vendor's salesroom or factory and may produce fresh merchandising ideas. The buyer must determine when to make such visits, basing his decision on past experience and on the likelihood of achieving worthwhile results.

The Handling of Clerical and Desk Work. These details can be extremely time-consuming and the greatest thief of the buyer's time. The amount of mail from vendors and stores, inter-office memos, executive pronouncements, changes of procedure, trade publications, price changes up and down, requests for return of merchandise, discrepancy-in-shipment reports, and so forth, is often overwhelming. Much of it requires thoughtful replies if communication is to be kept open and reciprocal. How efficiently the buyer handles this mountain of paper may well determine how much time will remain to him in his busy day to perform the more productive parts of his job. The training and development of his clerical staff and the use he makes of other available clerical facilities will help to keep this load under control.

The Setting of Priorities. Priorities must be established if the buyer is to use his time most effectively. Many buyers find it invaluable to be at their desks in advance of the arrival of the clerical staff and the opening of the office in order to schedule their day's activities and to establish the order of importance of what they hope to accomplish. Rare is the day that the full schedule is carried out, but a quiet time of planning before the phone begins to ring and other interruptions start will be most productive.

* * *

At the crossroads between the producer and the retailer, the buyer is in a most advantageous position to develop the broad point of view so important to executive action and higher-level responsibilities. Whether or not he moves on to other roles in or out of mass merchandising, the buyer will have gained valuable experience in responsible decision-making. And he will have acquired the discipline of operating in a goldfish bowl where all his purchasing errors are conspicuous and remembered until they are painfully marked down and sold out. He will have had a good education in the importance of communication of all kinds. He will have learned to work with and through many types of people. He will have become experienced in delegating work to others and in following up details. Other types of employment provide equally good training in many of these areas but none does it any better.

THE PLACE OF THE BUYER IN THE MODERN RETAIL ORGANIZATION

The modern-day buyer usually reports directly to a divisional merchandise manager responsible for the results in several related departments. The divisional merchandise manager in turn reports to a merchandising vice-president. A common breakdown of departments would be one divisional merchandise manager for housewares, one for apparel and one for the variety departments. The larger chains will have further breakdowns, while in the smaller chains, the merchandising vice president may also be the merchandise manager for all divisions. Major departments, which have a greater sales volume than the average department and therefore have a greater work load, may include senior buyers as well as associate or assistant buyers. Divisional merchandise managers in large chains may require extensive help from staff assistants in areas of merchandise control, planning, and procedures.

Thus, the organization of mass-merchandising buying divisions today varies considerably, depending upon the size of the company and the degree of store autonomy. But fundamentally, in any company, it is the *buyer's responsibility to choose, the divisional merchandise manager's responsibility to weigh, and the merchandising vice president's responsibility to balance.* Figure 1 is an organization chart that shows the position of a typical buyer in relation to the other sections of a retail chain.

The careful planning of organization setups and a breakdown of functions by individuals are essential to today's systematic and scientific management. Without the clear delegation of duties and responsibilities two things happen. First, there is an overlapping and duplication of effort as, for example, one buying division wanders into the merchandising of another or takes on functions properly assigned to sales promotion personnel. Second, there are likely to be areas where responsibility is neglected or not handled at all, particularly if it is a thorny or problem area. For example, unclear assignments may result in unchecked or inaccurate advertising copy, or in uneconomical transportation routings.

But whereas carefully designed organization charts can be a great boon to precise control of function by management, poorly constructed and obsolete charts, or charts rigidly applied, can do great damage. They must not build walls that discourage interaction. The handbag buyer with valuable color information for the upcoming season should not withhold it from others. ("Charlie the shoe buyer can dig up his own information.") Initiative must not be discouraged because the chart does not specifically show that a buyer should do such and such. ("I thought it was Joe's job to pick up the ball there. I didn't want to infringe.") Charts should be flexible enough to give the abler man plenty of room in which to operate and grow. ("I left the company because I felt hemmed in and really unable to do a job.") And charts must be implemented by management so that communications flow in all directions—up, down and across. Top management decisions must be told and sold to the lower echelons, not allowed to filter down inaccurately with the danger of misunderstanding and even resentment.

While it is essential that everyone know the limits of his authority and responsibility, charts should not attempt to nail down too many details. Those neat little squares on a typical chart are not nearly as precise as they look. The chart-maker may have had misgivings

206

himself about crowding certain functions into rigid areas. Staff and task requirements or other circumstances may have changed since the chart was devised. A new merchandising development or policy decision or personnel change may call for adjustments.

Organization charts must also be loose-fitting enough to accommodate individual people. If a square peg in a buying division is getting the job done well and can't seem to do it in exactly the usual way, perhaps management can work out some compromise that will not destroy his effectiveness by shoving him into a round hole. A good buying division is good because it is effective. Charts should channel but not restrict its activities.

Line and Staff Organizations

The modern "line" organization makes decisions based on facts and services provided by the "staff" group. Actual orders are issued from the top down in the line organization. The board of directors would be at the top of a typical line structure; the president, the vice president in charge of merchandising, the divisional merchandise manager, and the buyer would occupy the next four rungs in the hierarchy. Staff personnel serve the members of the line group in such advisory or specialized capacities as promotion, display, transportation, and so on. They are available in varying numbers, according to the importance of their function and the size of the company.

The interplay of line and staff organizations and the importance of their integration and cooperation may be illustrated by the way in which a retailer might handle the merchandising of one apparel item. The buyer goes to his meeting with the vendor of this item armed with essential information passed on to him by line personnel. He is thoroughly acquainted with his company's overall objectives as to type of store operated, type of customer to be appealed to, and the image to be supported. He has learned the relative importance to his company of the merchandise category to which he is considering adding the item in hand. The controller's division has set the model investment, the turnover goals, and the open-to-buy dollars. The buyer's merchandising superiors have already supplied him with his immediate sales and profit goals.

207

The Role of the Buyer in Mass Merchandising

FIGURE 1 Organization Chart
The Position of the Buyer in Relation to
Other Operations in a Typical Retail Chain

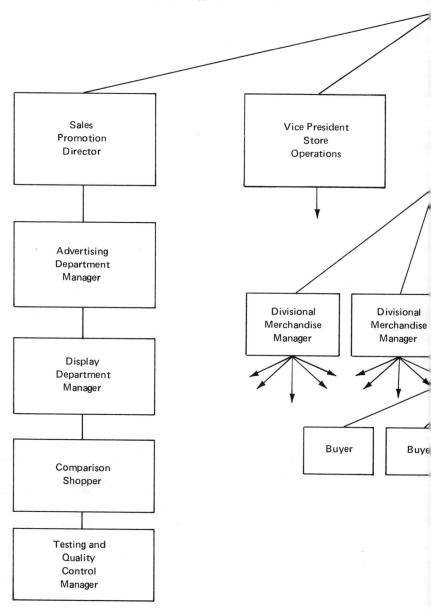

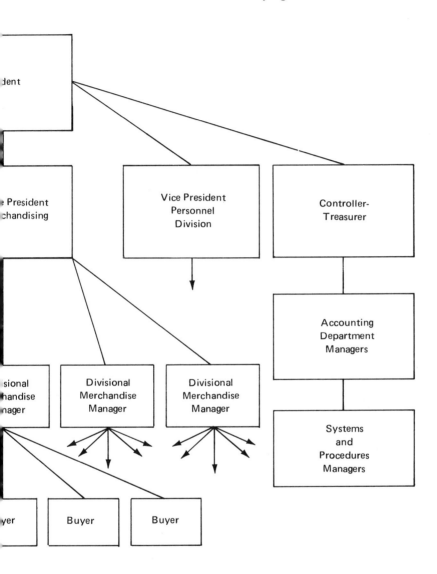

Moreover, he will have a definite sense of the adequacy of his present product mix in that category, the strengths and weaknesses of his selection, his values, and his price points.

Let us assume that the buyer has applied all of the above knowledge and experience to the apparel item under consideration and on the basis of this data, believes that its purchase will improve sales and profits. His final decision on the quantity and merchandising of the item may then be subject to the advice and direction of many others in his company. He will certainly discuss it and his plans for it with his immediate supervisor—a senior buyer and/or divisional merchandise manager. He will then consider how staff personnel can implement his purchase decision. He may consult the fashion coordinator about the styling or timeliness of the item. The transportation and warehousing divisions may be conferred with in reference to routing times and shipping costs. Perhaps the counsel of systems and procedure personnel would be needed to establish the best method of replenishing stocks of the item. And the buying-clerical staff must be called upon to produce the finished order. Thus, the interdependence of people in the buying operation and the necessity of maintaining wide-open lines of communication are evident even in this simple illustration.

The Importance of Good Communication

The buyer must be able to communicate in all directions. His knowledge and its timeliness, on which his effectiveness depends, must come from his suppliers and from store feedback. Information from manufacturers and other trade sources is available in quantities limited only by his own diligence. Communication between the buyer and the point of sale should be a regular, carefully-cultivated flow. The buyer is in a central position in this chain of communication. Though not a policy-maker, he can function as a good policy relayer and enforcer. As a reporter and interpreter of buying and selling information, he can be of great value.

But retailers, like other businessmen, or like scientists and philosophers, have developed a specialized jargon for communicating easily with each other. Much of their terminology and many of their abbreviations are only half understood by outsiders. The buyer who tries to communicate with salespeople and customers in that special language will probably not get through. "Corporate management tends to talk in a language comprehensible only to itself."[4] Buyers, like all other retailers, must speak and write with their audiences clearly in mind.

WOMEN AS BUYERS

According to a survey of 2,000 executives, retail trade was considered to be one of the few areas that permitted women equal access to management positions. The study showed the following breakdown of opinion on the subject of whether women enjoyed distinct advantages in retailing:[5]

	As Seen by Men	As Seen by Women
Distinct Advantage to Being a Woman	7%	11%
Equal	51%	46%
Moderate (but not equal)	37%	35%
Very Little	4%	4%
Virtually None	0%	0%

The same male executives who participated in this interview were of the opinion that women had much less access to management positions in other industries. Only a small percentage of these executives thought that women had equal opportunities in the following industries:

Financial Institutions	8%
Manufacturing—Consumer Goods	8%
Manufacturing—Industrial Goods	2%
Advertising, Media, Publishing	41%
Construction, Mining, Oil	0%
Defense or Space Industry	5%
Service Trades	21%
Transportation	4%
Public Utility	5%

[4] Warren J. Wittreich, "Misunderstanding the Retailer," *Harvard Business Review*, May-June 1962, p. 149.

[5] G. W. Bowman, N. B. Worthy and S. A. Greyser, "Are Women Executives People?" *Harvard Business Review*, July-August 1965, p. 14, Exhibit II.

211

Though the opinion of male executives on this subject may be highly questionable, it is clear that there is a general feeling that executive opportunities for women are much greater in retailing than in other industries. Consequently, opportunities for women in buying are also more plentiful.

Since the large majority of customers in retail stores are women (even in men's wear departments), women have a special contribution to make to merchandising at both the store and the buying level. Assuming equality of experience, education, and judgment, women are certain to have a deeper understanding of customer psychology—of why women buy and of what they buy. This understanding is especially valuable in such categories of merchandise as ladies' apparel and fashion accessories.

A woman buyer for a Missouri retail firm said: "I do believe that in the buying field, prejudice against women is less than in other areas. However, most of us stop there. Very few large stores have merchandise managers who are women. Posts above that are rarely held by women unless they are 'relatives.' "[6] There is no denying the existence of discrimination against women in any management position. A high percentage of men prefer to co-manage with other men. An even larger percentage do not like to be subordinate to a woman. But this bias is much less strong in the buying area of retailing, and it is diminishing as women continue to make greater contributions to the industry and to gain recognition for their achievements.

BUYER TRAINING

Mass merchandisers usually have highly developed and uniform store management training programs because a high percentage of their total personnel is actively employed in store operations and there is a need for the standardization of these functions. But most companies provide little formal buyer training, and even where some kind of fixed procedure does exist for the induction of the new buyer, it is often brief or hurried.

[6] *Ibid.,* p. 27.

212

Even highly organized companies are not likely to maintain a ready reservoir of buyers from which they can draw replacements when resignations, promotions, transfers, and dismissals occur. Retirements can be scheduled and planned, but most other changes in buying personnel are sudden. Regardless of the background of the new buyer, the need for training and orientation must be balanced against time limitations, the importance of maintaining a continuous flow of merchandise, and the routine operations of the department.

Formal training programs for new buyers tend to be neglected for a number of reasons. Such programs would have to be flexible enough to fit the new buyer with many years of experience in other capacities within the same company as well as the new buyer from another company with a background in entirely different areas. It would also have to accommodate the young man with no business experience of any kind. Newcomers to a company would need a much broader orientation program to perform effectively. As a result, mass-merchandising buyers are very often trained on the job. The trainee is frequently instructed to observe and operate in the shadow of either his predecessor or another buyer, or under the watchful eye of his divisional merchandise manager. The effectiveness of such an informal training program will depend on the skill of the teacher and on the amount of time he is willing to give to the new buyer.

However, a formalized schedule of buyer training and induction is highly recommended. Much of the success of mass merchandising rests on the principle of the standardization of proven methods and the execution of carefully planned programs and policies. Buyers should be initiated with the same care and precision with which store personnel are trained. A basic minimum orientation will be needed by all new buyers, regardless of background. A three-part program, including a preliminary interview, store operations orientation, and central office orientation, provides a good framework for the training of buyers and can be varied to suit the special requirements of individual companies.

The Role of the Buyer in Mass Merchandising

FIGURE 2.   Suggested Induction Schedule for New Buyers

1. Store Orientation*

A. Minimum of three months full-time at store or stores performing all duties connected with the selling, display, promotion, stock-keeping and replenishment of merchandise, with special attention to the categories that the trainee will buy.

B. Monthly progress reports by the trainee and the store manager to the divisional merchandise manager at the central office.

* This store phase of the induction schedule is, of course, waived for new buyers recruited from store operations.

2. Central Office Orientation

A. General interviews with the divisional merchandise manager, merchandising vice president and/or president on buying policies, company goals in general and the role of the buyer in accomplishing them.

B. Mornings of one week to be devoted to interviews with various division heads, followed by observation and discussion of division procedures. Afternoons to be devoted to working in the assigned buying divisions, although the trainee should touch base each day with his divisional merchandise manager or senior buyer to discuss the procedures he is observing and studying and to clarify their relevance to his buying role.

Observation of Office Division (mornings)

Controller's Division	Systems and procedures for the placing of orders, the paying of invoices, the control of investment, the production of statistical reports; financial controls and the functions of the computer.
Sales Promotion Division	Staff capabilities for promotion, advertising, display, sign-writing, and other techniques that help sell more merchandise.
Transportation Division	The routings available and the relative costs of each; their bearing on the buying and pricing of goods.
Warehousing Division	The advantages and disadvantages of warehousing in general, and, in particular, its usefulness for the buyer's special categories.

214

Personnel Division	The recruitment and training of all types of employees, with particular emphasis on the buying division.
Store Planning Division	The assignment of space, the layout and fixturing of new and remodeled stores; how these decisions are reached and the part played by the merchandising divisions in reaching them.

Buying Division Training (afternoons)

Order Writing	The mechanics of producing a printed or handwritten order for the exact quantities of merchandise and for the specific stores intended.
Correspondence "In"	Mail distribution, handling, and disposition.
Correspondence "Out"	Memo and letter writing, stenographic facilities.
Filing	Maintenance of quotation files for ready reference and of current statistical reports for quick availability.
Samples	Disposition of those kept and those discarded.
Forms	Their use, location, and requisition.
Telephone Service	Intra-office, local, and long-distance.
Markdown and Markup	Procedure for recording and approval.

By the end of a week, the buyer-trainee, especially if he has had some previous retail experience, should be taking an active part in all phases of his buying division's activities. The routines of central office orientation should be interrupted at any time that the trainee's attendance at any meeting or interview will be educational to him. During the training period, interviews with vendors should be held in conjunction with the new buyer's predecessor, senior buyer, or divisional merchandise manager until the buyer is ready to assume full responsibility.

Preliminary Interview

During the preliminary interview the buying position is offered, presumably accepted, and salary and benefits are agreed upon. The new buyer's prospective immediate superior, a representative of top management, and a personnel executive will usually be involved in this meeting. The buyer who is new to a company will, of course, require a more extensive orientation than an employee transferred from another part of the same firm. The induction schedule and its purposes will also be covered in detail at this time.

Store Operations Orientation

Unless the new buyer has had a solid background in store operations, he should be assigned a minimum of three months of full-time work at one or more stores. To make this period most meaningful, the buyer-trainee should actually perform all duties connected with the selling, display, promotion, stockkeeping, and replenishment of merchandise, with special attention paid to the categories he will buy. In addition, the trainee should work with and get to know store personnel. The actual routine to be followed should be an adaptation of the company's existing training program for store management employees, adjusted to fit the buyer-trainee's time schedule. A monthly report on the new buyer's progress at the store should be made to the divisional merchandise manager at the central office by the buyer-trainee and the store manager.

Central Office Orientation

The buyer-trainee now arrives at company headquarters fresh from a minimum of three months' experience on the firing-line at the store level. Since he is about to specialize in a type of merchandise and in a particular function, he needs to know the scope of his operations, his place on the organization chart, and his relationship to the line and staff personnel with whom he will work. If he has been a store operations "generalist" with considerable executive latitude, he may now be required to shift mental gears to a more organization-minded and limited area of specialization.

Even the new buyer who has had an extensive background in store operations has probably not considered many aspects of the buyer-store relationship that will become important when he begins to work in his unaccustomed capacity. Although the maintenance of a store point of view is important to good buying, the new buyer's decisions now affect more than one store. An error or misjudgment can now hurt every store and an effective bit of merchandising can benefit all stores rather than one.

Before the buyer-trainee starts out on his central office schedule of interviews and systems reviews, his divisional merchandise manager and/or merchandising vice president should brief him on the company's buying policies and goals in general and on his own role in accomplishing them. The buyer's special categories of merchandise should also be discussed at this time. Then he should proceed on his rounds to each division of the office. (See Figure 2.)

Some managements may maintain that such a schedule is too time-consuming and not really necessary. Since many merchants feel, with much justification, that paperwork and clerical routines absorb too much of their own time and that of their executives, they tend to underestimate the importance of a sound understanding of clerical procedures in liberating a buyer. But a new buyer wandering about an office with no clear idea as to how to perform a simple, everyday task, how to delegate clerical work, or how to locate information, becomes frustrated, ineffective, and a burden to others. With a solid grounding in both store and central office operations behind him, the new buyer will be in a much better position to move ahead effectively and to exercise good judgment in his more important work as a buyer.

ADVICE TO THE NEW BUYER

A change of job should be welcomed by anyone interested in mass retailing as a career. It is always a revitalizing experience and a chance to make a fresh start. Mistakes, failures, and bad personal relationships are left behind. The recruit is immediately challenged by an entirely new set of problems and a situation that stimulates learning and growth. Buoyed up by the knowledge that his

217

superiors have had enough confidence in him to promote him to his new job, the new buyer has the opportunity to take a giant step forward in his retailing career.

However, over-confidence should not lead the new buyer to seek self-sufficiency in decision-making too soon. He should avoid a "bull-in-a-china-shop" approach. Inexperience is to be expected on a new job. Ignorance of methods and procedures should not embarrass the newcomer or deter him from asking questions.

The new buyer's predecessor will no doubt have left some problems and negative conditions behind him, as the new buyer himself will most likely do when he moves on. These negative inheritances should be accepted without complaint as normal to most merchandising situations. The newcomer should learn from both the errors and the achievements of those who went before him.

The new buyer will immediately be snowed under by the attentions of all suppliers of his categories—those now selling to his company and those hopeful of making a fresh start with the new man. No immediate changes should be made, but the new buyer should listen carefully to all, since he will learn more about the merchandise he buys from vendors than from any other single source.

The new buyer should study all reports and statistics available to him and discuss them with his superiors. This will help him to pin down his position and to chart his course toward the goals he is striving to attain.

The new buyer must become acutely aware of what competitors are doing in his specialized area. He should develop this awareness by shopping competitive stores and by listening to and asking questions of suppliers. Only then will he be able to gauge the effectiveness of his own merchandise assortments and model stocks.

14

The Future of the Buyer's Role

Change, it has been said, is an ordeal. Still, I believe it will be precisely our ability to change that will give us the opportunity to capitalize on a mobile market and emerge as a leader . . . rather than a victim. [1]

Changes in consumer demand and changes brought about by the computer are taking place at a quickening pace. The buyer's role is extremely dependent on changes of all kinds. The buyer as well as all retailers must welcome change and take advantage of the challenges and opportunities it presents.

Trends in the total economy will influence the decisions of top management much more than they will those of the buyer, but he too will be much affected by the climate in which he works. Conditions that will directly or indirectly have a bearing on the buyer's daily activities and long-range planning include the following:

Customer Affluence. Per capita income is likely to continue to show a steady growth. As basics consume a smaller and smaller proportion of total income, the average customer's discretionary spending will increase, which means that more money will be available for impulse purchases and luxuries.

[1] Dorothy Pollack, Vice President-Advertising/Fashion, Formfit Rogers/Genesco, in an address at Dayton's, Minneapolis, Minnesota, March 10, 1969.

Population Growth. Any increases in population, of course, mean expanding markets. The retailer will follow the geographical growth patterns by setting up his outlets in the more densely populated areas. The suburbs are certain to be one of these growth areas.

Younger Consumers. Young adults represent a growing percentage of the total market. Their resistance to old values and old products, their conflict with the established and traditional, will force retailing, like all other institutions, to adapt.

Better Education. Better informed, more literate, more sophisticated customers will have to be approached and sold differently by retailers.

Consumerism. Customers will be more and more aware and they will be increasingly vocal and organized in expressing their dissatisfactions with retailing errors. They will expect more product information and better protection of their health and safety.

Growth in Productive Efficiency. It is anticipated that industry will continue to improve its efficiency and technology so that new products will appear in abundance and existing products will be brought within the reach of more consumers as costs are lowered.

Increased Leisure. Consumers who are working fewer hours per week will have more time for and interest in vacations, travel, entertainment, and personal care. Retailers and buyers will be alert to provide products and services in these growing areas.

Of course, unpredictable events such as wars will upset any crystal-ball gazing. A high rate of inflation will change the relationships of important factors involved in long-range planning. The only certainty is that the future of the economy, as it affects retailing and buying, will be volatile and variable. However, any attempt to control change must be preceded by an effort to achieve as much understanding of it as possible.

TRENDS WITHIN RETAILING

Forecasting, though treacherous, is an everyday function of management. Each buyer purchase is a preduction of its sales results, a calculated bet on its profitability. And although any developments within retailing may be canceled out by a shift in the economy as a whole, there will always be clues to the future in the faint trends that can already be identified.

The Big Will Continue to Grow Bigger

The growth rate of the giant chains is expected to persist. Increasing size will lead to greater specialization of function in merchandising and buying. For example, a combined men's and boys' wear division will be separated into its component parts, with distinct buying staffs that will bring greater skills to bear on the merchandising of each.

The big chains are not only expanding in numbers of stores, but they are also building larger units. Merchants who have made their mark in one area of retailing are crossing over into other areas as well. Food stores have penetrated into general merchandise, discounters have moved into fashion and other traditional department store areas. Department stores have entered the discount area, and variety stores are seeking to escape their low price-point image by merchandising higher-ticket lines. The attempt to win a larger share of the total retail market will continue through experimentation with new products and services.

From the customer's point of view, the trend to larger individual stores provides the convenience of one-stop shopping—being able to fill all or a high percentage of her needs under one roof with a minimum of transportation and parking problems and as quickly as possible. But the future of this "all-things-to-all-people" trend is not at all clear. Customer convenience can turn into inconvenience if the dimensions of a store become too vast. Walking distances between one wanted category and another may seem too great, and customers may not feel at home in such spacious surroundings.

Customers may also become puzzled and unhappy in a store that has no distinct image. Movement away from the specialized form of

221

retailing, on which a chain's success was built, to a more general style, may weaken the company's total appeal. When a discounter abandons aggressive price reductions, he creates opportunities for specialty discounters to move in and take over that business. Variety chains permitted much of their health and beauty aids business to be siphoned off when they chose not to meet the low-pricing of small discounters operating from low-rent, sidestreet locations.

Consumers with more leisure time may also become less interested in one-stop shopping and be more diverted by stores that specialize in everything for the skier, the boatman, the knitter, or the home gardener. The only thing that can be predicted with any assurance is that the consumer will be the one to shape the future in all areas. The retailer and buyer must listen closely to her preferences and remain as flexible as possible in their attitudes and decisions.

Planning Versus Scrambling

"Buyers are still creatures of the moment with a stocklist in one hand, a weather map in the other. Any plan goes out the window with a late season, bad weather, etc. . . . There literally are only two forms of management—management by plan and management by crisis. No industry can profitably survive in tomorrow's economy without long range planning done and implemented by top management—the scramblers will not be in the ball game."[2]

The buyer of the future will increasingly find that he is an integral part of a comprehensive retailing and marketing plan that includes investment management, display, sales promotion, store operations and design, transportation, and warehousing. The short-range goal of "beating-this-week's-sales-last-year" will tend to be replaced by a longer-range look at the position of the retailer or buyer in relation to his plan for a full season. This inclusive plan will cover not only sales, but all aspects of merchandise and money control as well.

[2]A. Stuart Powell, Jr., Editor, *Department Store Management,* December 1968, p. 15.

The integration of all phases of retailing that will result from planning instead of scrambling will encourage the comprehensive analysis of specific merchandising trends, including the further exploration of shop, boutique, or "total merchandising." Total merchandising has been defined as "the segmentation of consumer markets by buying motive, not by need; the recognition of these motives by merchants and their capitalization with items; and the inter-connection of these items, so that they have a marketing vitality together that is greater than what they would have individually."[3] Total merchandising clearly calls for a team approach in which the buyer would participate.

Self-service will continue to affect the development of merchandising. As wage costs continue to mount, audio-visual devices will replace people, and there will be an even greater need for packaging that sells the product by dramatizing its uses and satisfaction. Home-shopping by TV may become important; the consumer will sit down with her shopping list before a two-way television device that will enable her to buy without ever leaving her home.

Several developments in the area of improved communications are also likely to result from longer-range planning. Total merchandising concepts will surely lead to closer working relationships with manufacturers in an attempt to establish goals for the future. Retailers who plan ahead will be more curious about what their competitors are doing and more interested in working out common problems with them. And mass merchandisers will pay more and more attention to social and community affairs; this responsibility, already recognized and accepted, will require a great deal of implementation, both at the buying office and at local levels.

Electronic Data Processing

The great potential benefits of the computer to merchandising have hardly been realized. But the attention and monies that are already being invested in EDP will surely and increasingly bear

---

[3]Joseph T. Moran, Jr., of Sears, Roebuck & Co., as quoted in *Department Store Management*, March 1970, p. 61.

fruit. Retailers and their buying staffs will learn not only how to read the statistical output and reports of the computers, but also how to use them creatively to function more effectively and profitably. The ability to analyze and use the computer's data will gradually catch up with the ability to capture them. EDP will be wholeheartedly accepted by merchants as a helpful ally rather than resisted as a puzzling mechanism. Its truly great value in providing quick and accurate reports of what the customer wants will be fully recognized and acted on by the retailer and buyer.

It is also likely that the limitations of computers will be better understood. Excessive fascination with technique and neat mathematical statements will diminish through trial and error. Merchandising will still require thought and intuition. The buyer's role will be that of coping with the un-programmable and implementing what can be programmed.

Electronic data processing as applied to retailing makes possible a new and higher degree of standardization—in buying, in display, and in the determination of model stocks and merchandise assortments. But the possibly stifling effects of rigid standardization on individual store initiative and morale will be increasingly recognized too. As the average store becomes large enough to afford more management, it will become more capable of adapting to local demands and conditions and avoid the facelessness of an over-standardized operation.

THE BUYER OF THE FUTURE

By providing selling information more rapidly, more completely, and more accurately than ever before, electronic data processing will give the buyer more time to produce—to develop ideas and to merchandise them. EDP will give him detailed information on *what* has happened to an item he bought; it will remain for him to find out *why* it has happened.

The buyer will be in a better position to do, or to assist in doing, a "total merchandising" job. The increasing size of the typical mass-merchandising operation has probably led to buying specialization, to a concentration on fewer categories of merchandise. The buyer, therefore, becomes more of an expert. He not only will be more in touch with results, but will also be more market-oriented, and spend more time at factories, showrooms, and competitive stores. He will be a better money-management engineer than his predecessors, producing better turnover and better return on his company's investment.

Hopefully, the buyer of the future will be freer to manage his operations on a higher level—to develop pretesting techniques; to blend his basics and his promotional goods in a merchandise mix that will consistently produce the planned net profit; and even sometimes to do the unusual and unorthodox that represent real personal achievement. "Often the margin of advantage over a competitive store is very slight—just the difference that *care in selection and support of suppliers* will make." [4] The better buyer is the one who has the capacity and opportunity to win this margin of advantage for his company.

But no matter how different the future face of retailing will be, one thing will not change. No system, regardless of the wonders of the computer, despite more perfect planning, will be able to foretell accurately the preferences and demands of the consumer. In fact, it is safe to predict that the present huge, concerted effort toward scientific, programmed, computerized merchandising will overreach its mark by neglecting to listen closely enough to the customer. The big retailer today is in danger of organizing for more turnover, smaller investment, thinner backup stocks, and lower store operations costs to the point where the customer may be alienated and sent elsewhere. Tomorrow's successful mass merchandisers and buyers will clearly be the ones who can not only achieve better control of their operations through mechanization and planning, but can also keep in close touch with their customers and tailor their programs to their shifting demands.

The shopper of the future will be better informed, less easily satisfied, more outspoken, and more affluent. Seated in his remote office, the buyer of the future will need more than ever to com-

[4]Charles G. Taylor, "How to Work with Resources," *The Buyer's Manual, op. cit.*, p. 74.

municate with his customers, to acquire and maintain an understanding of their points of view. As the specialist and best-informed person in his merchandise categories, it is and will be his role to so research his particular area that he truly becomes the purchasing agent for customers in the communities where his company's stores are located. "Buy low, sell high, collect damn quick . . . is a frank, concise statement of a product-oriented 'Get rid of the body' philosophy. The needs of the customer, however, both primary and ultimate, are somewhat conspicuous by their absence."[5]

Tomorrow's successful retailer and buyer will try with every contact to participate in the communities in which they operate, to demonstrate friendliness, consideration, and understanding. The buyer can achieve such rapport through the choice and development of products of good design, quality, and safety, through adequate merchandise selection and depth of stocks, through timely purchase and delivery of wanted items, and through advertising that describes accurately and forcefully. The successful buyer of the future will know local consumer needs and how he can best satisfy them. He will recognize ethnic variances and adjust his assortments accordingly. He will understand that increased customer affluence and leisure time have created the opportunity to make shopping a pleasant, satisfying experience rather than simply the chore of replenishing basic needs in a big hurry.

The successful mass-merchandising buyer of the future will be the one who lifts his nose from the grindstone high enough and long enough to view his role in some perspective. He will be the one who is alert to the ordeal of change, who sees himself as an important member of a total merchandising team, who is ever mindful of his customers' needs and satisfactions.

[5]Matt Wigginton, Director of Genesco Inc., in an address to the International Fashion Market, Montreal, Canada, May 26, 1967.

Glossary of Retailing Terms[1]

assortment, the selection of goods available to customers.

brand, a name that identifies the merchandise of one company exclusively.

broker, an agent representing either the buyer or seller who does not physically own or control the merchandise.

cash discount, an allowance granted to the retailer for payment within a specified time period.

category, a natural grouping of merchandise with the same broad appeal to and use by customers.

chain store, one of a group of homogeneous retail outlets that is centrally owned, and usually centrally operated.

classification, "a segment of customer demand . . . made up of homogeneous items, reasonably substitutable for one another in the customer's eyes.[2]

---

[1]This Glossary provides broad definitions of words and terms commonly used in retailing and in this text. For more exact definitions of greater concern to controllers and accountants, see *Mass Merchandisers' Guide to Sales and Expense Reporting* (New York: Mass Merchandising Research Foundation, April 1969); *Retail Accounting Manual,* 1962 Controllers Congress, National Retail Merchants Association; *Report of the Definitions Committee, The Journal of Marketing,* October 1948.

[2]Frank Burnside, "Merchandising by Classification," *The Buyer's Manual, op. cit.,* p. 181.

department store, a retail store that merchandises a very wide assortment of products and is organized by separate departments to sell, promote, and offer service in those various categories of merchandise. Its price ranges are usually higher than those of variety and discount stores.

discount store, a store "that is over 10,000 square feet, with both hard and soft goods departments, and with a cost structure below that of a traditional store."[3]

franchise, an exclusive privilege to sell particular products, granted by a supplier to a retailer.

gross margin, the difference between the cost of merchandise and its selling price.

inventory, stock of goods on hand at retail value.

investment, inventory plus merchandise on order.

jobber, a middleman who buys from producers and sells to retailers.

landed cost, cost of merchandise plus transportation costs.

leased department, a department operated by someone other than store ownership.

mail-order house, a retailing company that receives orders and sells by mail.

manufacturer's agent or representative, one who contracts with a manufacturer or distributor to sell a product or line to a restricted group of customers or in a restricted area but is not exclusively employed by that manufacturer.

markdown, a reduction below the original retail selling price.

marketing, all business activities concerned with the movement of goods from the manufacturer to the ultimate user.

markon, the difference between the cost of the merchandise and its initial retail price, usually expressed as a percentage of the retail price.

markup, an increase in the initial retail price and markon on an item.

merchandising, that part of marketing which covers the selection, packaging, pricing, promotion, and display of goods, as well as the planning of quantities to be purchased and the timing of their delivery.

[3] *Discount Store News,* August 24, 1970, p. A-14.

net profit or loss, gross margin less total expense.

net sales, gross sales less returns and allowances.

open-to-buy, a specified amount of dollars available for purchases of a merchandise category within a fixed period of time, determined by the relationship of sales to inventory established in a merchandise plan.

overage, amount by which a physical inventory exceeds the inventory expected by bookkeeping methods.

private brand, a retailer's brand, sponsored by the seller rather than by the manufacturer.

programmed merchandising, a planned campaign to sell more merchandise, which uses the combined abilities of the manufacturer and the retailer's merchandising and promotional staffs, as contrasted with everyday item buying.

retailer, the person in the marketing process who sells directly to the ultimate consumer.

sales promotion, all supplementary activities that help to sell merchandise, such as display, advertising, publicity, and demonstration, as well as the coordination of all these activities.

shrinkage, unexplained differences between "book" inventories and "physical" inventories—between what should be on hand and what is on hand.

specialty store, a retail outlet that restricts its appeal to one type of merchandise to which it brings prestige and exclusiveness; specialty stores usually offer wider assortments in a narrower range than department, discount, or variety stores.

stock turn, see turnover.

trade discounts, allowances granted to the retailer, other than those given to encourage prompt payment.

turnover, the number of times that the inventory is replenished within a specified period of time, calculated by dividing the average inventory into the annual sales for that period.

variety store, a retail store that merchandises a very wide assortment of products, usually in price ranges below those of most department stores.

wholesaler, see jobber.

working capital, total current assets less total current liabilities.

Index

Neaman, Sam, 59
Nelson, Donald, 11
"Net impression" of advertising,
190-191
Net profit statement, 113-114
New products, 46, 55-58
consideration for, 57-58
failure rate of, 56
in model stocks, 78-79
test-marketing of, 56-57
youth market and, 56
New Products Action Team, Inc.,
56*n*, 57
J. J. Newberry Company, 141

One-stop shopping, 29, 222
Open-to-buy budget, 119-121
Optical scanning computer
input, 96
Order writing by computer, 99-100,
119
Organization charts, 206-207,
208 fig.
Out-of-stock conditions
computer analysis of, 99
merchandise assortment and,
47-48
turnover and, 122
Over-diversification, 50-51
Overhead costs
model stocks and, 73
in self-service, 116
Overstocking, 117

Packaging, 60-64
buyer's role in, 60, 61-62, 64
consumer convenience in, 62-63
inner-packing in, 13
legislation on truth in, 187-189
private brand, 60, 61-62, 180,
182-183
product appeal and, 60-61

self-service and, 12-13, 42, 61
for shipping, 13, 63
shrinkage and, 36
size in, 63-64, 70
supermarket development of, 61
vendor responsibility for, 12, 13,
60
for warehousing, 13, 63
J. C. Penney
private brands of, 171, 180
public affairs department of,
195
Pilferage *see* Shrinkage
Plan-o-gram, 142-145, 146 fig.
Pollack, Dorothy, 219*n*
Powell, A. Stuart, Jr., 222*n*
Prefabricated displayers, 147, 149
Pre-ticketing, 89
Price
advertising of, 190-191
"coverage game" and, 38-39
cutting of, 115-116
legislation on, 189
model stocks and line of, 66-67,
74-75, 82
of private brands, 179, 180
in promotions, 157
Private brands, 170-184
advantages of, 171-173
basic buying in, 181-183
customer loyalty and, 172-173,
179-180, 184
customer suspicion of, 179-180
development of, 179-180
discounting and, 172
display of, 184
future of, 183-184
hidden expenses of, 175-176
infringement and, 178
items suitable for, 176-178
management control of, 172
in model stocks, 77
national brands vs., 173-176, 178

Kirtley Library
Columbia College
8th and Rogers
Columbia, MO. 65201

DATE DUE

MAR 2 7 '77			
OCT 30 '77		OCT 1 4 1979	
NOV 25 '78	SEP 1 7 1979	OCT 1 7 1979	
JUL 25 '79	SEP 1 7 1979	NOV 1 1979	
SEP 5 '79	SEP 1 7 1979	NOV 0 7 1979	
AUG 3 1 1979	SEP 1 7 1979	NOV 2 6 1979	
SEP 4 1979	SEP 1 8 1979	DEC 1 8 1979 MAY 1 0 85	
P 5 1979	SEP 1 8 1979		
SEP 5 1979	SEP 1 8 1979	OCT 2 5 84	
SEP 1 0 1979	SEP 1 8 1979	NOV 7 84	
	SEP 1 9 1979	DEC 5 84	
SEP 1 0 1979	SEP 1 9 1979	NOV 25 94	
SEP 1 1 1979	SEP 1 9 1979	DEC 1 4 1998	
	SEP 1 9 1979		
SEP 1 1 1979			
SEP 1 3 1979	SEP 20 79		
SEP 1 7 1979	SEP 2 0 1979		
SEP 1 7 1979	SEP 2 1 1979		
SEP 1 7 1979	SEP 2 3 1979		

GAYLORD | | | PRINTED IN U.S.A.